Intertwingle
A compelling story of
what is possible

By
Judy Breck

With a foreword by Howard Rheingold

Judy Breck, Publisher
330 East 85th Street, Apt. 1B
New York NY 10028 USA
On the Internet: GoldenSwamp.com

First Edition: March 2008

ISBN: 978-0-6151-9919-1

In memory of my parents Julia and Louis Breck
who were routinely first to see the gorillas

CONTENTS

Preface

My Mother was a post-feminist way back in 1961 when she ran for Mayor of El Paso, Texas, got into a run-off, and lost by a squeaker to her male opponent. During the campaign, someone came up with the slogan "What the heck, vote for Breck," and it stuck. Mother was a mid-twentieth century post-feminist in this sense: her passion was not electing a woman, but bringing about what she called "good government." The slogan captured the idea perfectly: vote for Julia Breck because she is the best candidate—in spite of the fact that she is a woman!

I often tell her seven grandsons that it is a shame they did not have a chance to know her well. As young teenagers they were her pallbearers at her funeral, that overflowed with El Pasoans of all sorts. As I greeted the incoming crowd, I realized that Mother had been close to each in one or more of their endeavors.

Under the glass on the top of her dresser, Mother kept a cartoon showing a duck reacting to a firecracker in three different ways. In the first drawing, on the left, the firecracker is exploding under the duck's back end as feathers fly and he looks surprised. In the middle the duck is standing safely back watching the firecracker explode. In the third drawing, the duck is reaching out with a lighted match touching the fuse to cause the firecracker to ignite and blow up.

Mother's cartoon, that was there for her to look at every morning as she prepared for the day, had these three lines under the respective drawings:

Some of us don't know what happened.
Some of us watch what happens.
Some of us make things happen.

I wrote this book for all three kinds of ducks. The firecracker at the heart of the stories is the mobile computer. Whether you are losing some feathers, studying the situation, or helping hands-on, reading these stories will give you some background, vocabulary, and sketches of what the world will be like after the mobile explosion does its work.

My thanks to Ajit Jaokar who asked me to write a book about mobiles. My deep appreciation to Howard Rheingold for his encouragement and the Foreword. To Ted Nelson, thank you for your good humor in my adopting your wonderful word intertwingle.

Foreword

South of San Francisco and north of Silicon Valley, near the place where the pines on the horizon give way to the live oaks and radiotelescopes, an unlikely subculture has been creating a new medium for human thought. When mass-production models of present prototypes reach our homes, offices, and schools, our lives are going to change dramatically.

The first of these mind-amplifying machines will be descendants of the devices now known as personal computers, but they will resemble today's information processing technology no more than a television resembles a fifteenth-century printing press. They aren't available yet, but they will be here soon. Before today's first-graders graduate from high school, hundreds of millions of people around the world will join together to create new kinds of human communities, making use of a tool that a small number of thinkers and tinkerers dreamed into being over the past century.

Nobody knows whether this will turn out to be the best or the worst thing the human race has done for itself, because the outcome of this empowerment will depend in large part on how we react to it and what we choose to do with it. The human mind is not going to be replaced by a machine, at least not in the foreseeable future, but there is little doubt that the worldwide availability of fantasy amplifiers, intellectual toolkits, and interactive electronic communities will change the way people think, learn, and communicate.

I wrote the words quoted above in 1983, before the first Macintosh introduced graphical user interfaces and turned personal computers into appliances. Sometimes, you can see large aspects of the future by looking at smaller aspects of the present. One of the best ways to practice this kind of foresight is to look at new intersections of technologies with each other and with social trends. For example, if I saw what the researchers at Xerox PARC were doing with the first microprocessors and television screens in the 1970s, and I knew something about the projected cost-effectiveness of microchips, put that technological knowledge together with what I knew about the increasing importance of information in business, education, and private life, and pieced together a fairly accurate picture of what life would be like a quarter century hence. Again, if you were one of the thousands of people who connected our telephones to our personal computers with modems and logged into computer bulletin boards in the mid 1980s, you might have had a notion about the way people might use the Internet when the hybrid computer-telephone technology matured in the late 1990s. Judy Breck is looking at something similar today, and piecing together a picture of yet another kind of future, by looking at the way personal computing, the mobile telephone, the Internet, and vast multimedia collections of knowledge are beginning to intersect with education.

As the poet Muriel Rukeyser noted, "the universe is made of stories, not atoms." Although the silicon microprocessors and optical communication networks make up the infrastructure for tomorrow's global education system, Breck wisely uses the lens of stories, rather than dry descriptions of technologies, to bring into view the "perfect storm" that is brewing in education. It doesn't take a lot of convincing to persuade us that most of the people in the world are going to be carrying or wearing a powerful mobile communication device ten years from now -- there are already three billion mobile phones in the world, and the computers in today's gaming machines are already tens of thousands more powerful than the supercomputers of previous eras. And it is becoming increasingly clear that in a globalized, networked world, education is the most important socioeconomic survival skill that persons and nations will require. In most of the world, sadly, social capacity to deliver a 21st century education is deteriorating, not expanding and evolving. The economic costs of schools, teachers, and curricular materials are soon going to cease to be barriers in important ways, as open educational materials like MIT's Open Courseware become available for the cost of telephone access to billions of people. But how will this technological capability be developed? Technologies do not autonomously dictate how they will be used. Humans and institutions grapple with, appropriate, redesign, adopt, reject, evolve technologies -- particularly when the technologies enable people to apply our particularly powerful capabilities of thought and social communication.

How might the world of 2030 look if enough people were to understand the possibilities that coming technologies enable, and to create or repurpose our social and political institutions to take full advantage of m-learning? What if billions of people were able to attain more of their potential -- something we're going to need in order to solve the problems we've created for ourselves? A compelling story of what is possible, a clear image of a desirable future, may wield decisive power in these, the early days of the smartmob era.

— Howard Rheingold

Intertwingle
**A word for new things going on
that we have not had a word for**

This book explores a new kind of world which people too young to remember before the Internet era will experience through their lifetime. It is a virtual world that has already begun to emerge. This place within a global cloud of connectivity is becoming increasingly novel, as it overcomes 20th century efforts to conform it to old ways of communicating and handling information.

Completely new ways of doing these things are taking shape. Those born into it understand what is happening intuitively because what has changed for those of us who are older has always been there for them. The new generation is growing up with the virtual world at their fingertips and, as their mobile devices become more and more sophisticated, in their pockets.

A grand global adventure is underway as the virtual world emerges. Novel things take place there—new things go on that we have not had a word for. To give those things a name, I use a word in this book that has been around for three decades, but pretty much ignored until recently when the insight it points to has become more obvious.

The word is intertwingle. I found it in Peter Morville's book Ambient Findablility,[1] where Morville uses it as a chapter title. Under the title on the first page of the chapter are these words:

> Intertwingularity is not generally acknowledged—people keep pretending they can make things deeply hierarchical, categorizable and sequential when they can't.
> Everything is deeply intertwingled.
> —Theodor Holm Nelson

Ted Nelson, an early pioneer of information technology who coined the word hypertext way back in 1964. In 1974 Nelson coined intertwingle when he wrote in Computer Lib/Dream Machines[2] that "everything is intertwingled."

Over the thirty-plus years since he made the above comment, most of the computer crowd have gone right on doing what Ted Nelson said: pretending they can build a virtual world designed around hierarchies, categories and sequences. Their efforts are at the root of widespread frustration suffered by

---

1 Peter Morville. *Ambient Findability.* O'Reilly, 2005, p. 64.
2 http://en.wikipedia.org/wiki/Intertwingularity#CITEREFNelson1974

computer users. Moving up and down a nest of file folders inside of file folders inside of still more file folders is a hierarchal horror. Databases and table formats are category prisons. With the exception of the interjection of hyperlinks here and there, text used in the digital world has been relentlessly sequential.

In the past dozen years the Internet has emerged with uncountable spontaneous connections. Nonetheless, websites have been assumed from early on to be hierarchies with a homepage at the top and nests of categories below that, with sequences of related content. But that kind forcing of hierarchies, categories and sequences is now breaking down. Websites, on their own, have interconnected internally and with each other ignoring the old paper-world rules.

The computerese language I have been using just means the computer crowd has pushed, pulled and jumped through hoops to try to make the virtual world act like the two-dimensional, world of paper communication and storage. But things are now changing: the omni-dimensional natural structure of the networked online virtual world is pushing aside these mistakes. The inevitable failure of the false efforts is surfacing, allowing intertwingularity to show off its powers and beauty.

In the social world that young people are beginning to build with their mobiles, hierarchies, categories and sequences are minimal. My faves are intertwingled with your faves and each of us touches and is touched in ways that cannot be shoehorned into the simple little patterns of the paper past. There is very little in Flickr or MySpace that can be pinned down into hierarchies, categories or sequences. Most everything is intertwingled.

As I have been using the word intertwingle here, my guess is that the word itself gives you an idea of what I am using it to describe. Intertwingle is not in the dictionary so far, but what is going on within the new virtual world is not yet a very well defined science and lacks a precise vocabulary. Intertwingle is a word I use in these pages to mean the new ways of the virtual world, and how they may reflect some of the networked basis of the tangible world.

The chapters ahead include the names of concepts that are parts of the big intertwingling in which the youngest generation is increasingly engaged. The book explores these in four sections: *Connecting, The New Place, Intertwingularities* and *Learning*. I hope your journey through them will be an interesting look into the mechanisms that are forming. As you think about what is happening, I believe you will join me in being a joyful enthusiast for what we can expect: what is coming is, to use a new generation adjective, awesome.

Ted Nelson has told us that intertwingled is something that the world itself is, and is deeply. It is fascinating, and I think true, to realize that in the new virtual world we are encountering echoes of the deeply intertwingled nature of reality. The unnatural one-way media of radio and television that blasted at populations throughout the 20th century tended to crumble cultures and numb individual initiative and creativity. As the interactive Internet—increasingly held in individual hands—lets us intertwingle with information and each other it will be the tyranny and its terror that will be diminished.

A lot of people these days are apprehensive of a future that they imagine as a global tectonic shift of peoples and nations, fraught with radical dangers. The pages ahead will give you a very different picture. Tyranny and terror are hierarchical, categorical and sequential; they will wither in the global human intertwingularity that emerges in the connectivity cloud enveloping our planet.

The chapters ahead give you a new way to think about the future. To make the concepts plainer and to let your toy with them in some fictional context, each chapter begins by looking in on some people who would now be children or teenagers. When we meet them in the stories, they are thirty-somethings, living in the future. We begin in the year 2030 in a hothouse in Rwanda.

CONNECTING
Entering and participating in the new virtual world of digital connectivity

The Eight Hundred Pound Gorilla

Aframomum Hothouse
May 2030

Shema and Margarita had kept in virtual touch since their intern time together a decade ago. She was genuinely thrilled to be at last walking through the airlocks to observe for herself Shema's pinnacle paradise plants. She was particularly excited to be able to see—and if he kept his promise—touch his prize Aframomums.

As she pushed through out of the final cleaning air chamber, Shema stepped up to give her a welcoming high five. The two have a lot in common. They were both born in 2000 and had each become fascinated with growing things when they were small children. Margarita grew up in New Mexico's Rio Grande River Valley where her father was the foreman of a large chili farm. In return for his promise to let her touch his Aframomum, Shema had made Margarita agree not only to bring some of her father's chilies along on her trip, but to cook a Mexican meal during her stay. He was also silently hoping that Margarita would show his wife some of the secrets of Mexican cooking.

As a twenty-first century Rwandan child, Shema had ridden the wave of determination in that country to use technology training to overcome the nation's deficit of natural resources. By the time he was twelve-years-old Rwanda was living up to its informal nickname as Africa's "ICT Alley," and Shema's learning level rivaled that of children his age who were enjoying the best of educations on other continents.

While the majority of young Rwandans his age were lured in their teens into tech careers in the booming "Alley," Shema scoured the Internet for information about botany and horticulture. He jumped into discussion groups and wikis, where he became a popular contributor because he always seemed to come up with something about a rare—often weird—African species.

It was through the *World Wiki of Wonderful Spices* that Shema's career path began. He started reading the Grains of Paradise section, which at the time he first logged in was mainly developing historical themes. Shema knew that Aframomum, which was part of the *Grains of Paradise* group had become the most promising anti-inflammatory drug yet discovered.

"Wow, guys," Shema typed into the wiki back channel, "it may be interesting that Aframomum was caravanned across the ancient Sahara, but the coolest aspect is it most likely kept the camel drivers from having heart attacks." As usual, Shema had stirred up the conversation.

But one reply he received by direct email got his full focus. It was from the pharmaceutical company that was developing Aframomum-based medicines. He was being offered a prime apprenticeship and he accepted. At age fourteen Shema went to work, learning and contributing to one of the most effective life-saving substances ever found. His employer spared no expense in underwriting his education as he finished his teens and took a doctorate. By age thirty, as he hosted Margarita in his hothouse facility, Shema was recognized as the world's leading Aframomum scientist.

Although her business card title says "Cuisine Specialist," Margarita was in 2030 and just about always had been a cook. Through the three decades of her lifetime, as technology and the virtual world became bigger and bigger, the hands-on cooking craft became more and more highly prized. By age 28, Margarita held a top faculty position at the Spaceport Culinary Institute located in southern New Mexico. In charge of teaching the preparation and cooking of legumes, she liked to call herself "Dean of Beans."

Its location at the Spaceport worked in three ways to put the institute into global prominence. As the ever-faster vehicles being developed to explore space began to make quick jumps among airports around the world, the institute was able to ship hot meals to Paris, St. Petersburg, Cairo, Beijing—any major city—to be consumed at six-star restaurants within half a day. Once that service began, the institute established its own six-star restaurant which was frequented by intercontinental diners. The third plus for the location was the very old one that the nearby Rio Grande Valley was an ideal growing area for spices, especially for chili. As has been true for several centuries, it was impossible to find a better Mexican food meal anywhere than Las Cruces, New Mexico.

In pursuing her studies of legume preparation, Margarita developed a theory linking the use of spices as a medicinal as well as palate-pleasing skill. As a teen-ager she made a suggestion now and then for the Wikipedia article on chili. As chili began to play an increasing role in lowering insulin spikes in pre-diabetics, Margarita took a one-year side trip in her cooking studies to intern in a phar-maceutical laboratory where she participated in experiments with the capsaicin ingredient in chili.

The company where Margarita interned was the same one that had taken Shema on as an apprentice. The year she spent in Delaware at the company's laboratory, Shema was also assigned there. They were twenty-years-old and lonely for home, where each had left behind a fiancé. While both kept romanti-cally in touch with their spouses-in-waiting, a wonderful friendship grounded in deeply shared intellectual interests developed between Margarita and Shema.

The high-five from Shema as Margarita entered his hothouse was followed by a bear hug. Then Margarita began to scan the space and fill her nostrils with the smorgasbord of scents. The glass-ceilinged room was lined with tables into which were set open containers about twenty inches in diameter across the top. The lower portions of the containers narrowed to "v" shapes and had rows of short slits along the sides. The containers were filled with soil in which Shema's plants were growing.

"Shema," Margarita said, "are those plants growing in computer monitors?"

"Yes they are," he replied. "The glut of the things makes them not only free. The ICT companies paid us, along with anyone else they could find who would put them to use. Then they put it in their advertising that they were recycling."

"Do you use the CRT tubes too?" she asked.

"No," he said. "I think those get ground up by some fiberboard company that makes insulated wallboards. But we do use the CPU cases, let me show you." He took her to a back section of the hothouse where the rectangular boxes that once had held desktop computer central processing units now contained multiple rows of seedlings.

Margarita looked puzzled. "Shema, there hasn't been a desktop computer made for fifteen years. You may have to go back to wooden boxes ones of these days."

"Actually, the ones you see here are the last batch we have. When everything went mobile back in the early teens, Rwanda was ahead of the tech curve. We just cleared the desktops out and went 100% wireless by 2013. You guys back in the States took longer, I know."

"I'm afraid you're right," the Dean of Beans said with a frown.

"Let me show you where we keep our prize Grains of Paradise—the Aframumum bioclone," Shema said with a broad smile, and pointing over his shoulder.

They walked to the back of the hothouse and made their way through another set of airlock doors. The chamber they entered was much larger than the first one. It was a swamp, with high humidity and rain falling. Margarita asked with surprise in her voice, "You raise your precious crop outdoors?"

"We've fooled you, and I hope the plants are fooled too. For sure, they are happy here. Their flowers are an average of twenty percent larger than they are in the Liberian lowlands we emulate in here." He went on to explain that remote sensors were placed in a grid in a two-acre area of swamp in Liberia—a place where the Aframomum plants thrive. "Whatever happens there happens here,"

7

Shema said, "We are getting wet right now because it was raining yesterday in Liberia."

He pulled his mobile out of his pocket and offered to stop the rain.

"My Navajo grandfather would call you rain god! I am very impressed," she responded. "Just find me an umbrella." They both laughed as he handed her one and she popped it open. "We don't get much moisture in New Mexico," Margarita said, "and I really do enjoy the rain."

By 2030, when Shema was showing Margarita his prize Aframomum melegueta, bioclone pods were sprouting up in many parts of the planet, and plans were underway to build three of them on the moon. The pods are sealed environments, usually five to ten acres in size. The soils, flora and fauna used on the inside floor of a pod are either natural and very much like a distant location to be cloned or—in the most expensive of the pods—actual dirt, plants and animals moved to the pod from the cloned spot.

Within the sealed pod, the weather occurring at the distant location is cloned. The cloning is done by reconstruction of actual weather at the remote location with a one-day delay to the creation of identical weather within the bioclone pod. The information for exactly copying the remote weather is gathered by pooling data from satellites, remote sensors and any causal sources such as from the mobiles carried by visitors who happen to be in the cloned area. Numerous plants and animals at the remote location also are patched with mobiles that transmit data about these living inhabitants.

Shema escorted Margarita along the elevated visitors pathway into the swamp. They stopped at a gate in the heavy-gauge wire enclosure that surrounded the walkway. Shema pointed his mobile at a small panel near the gate handle and the gate swung open. He led Margarita down three steps to the muddy swamp ground, where she realized that they were surrounded by Aframomum melegueta plants. Not only could she touch them, they were touching her. "This," she thought, "is true paradise for a spice specialist."

Shema urged her to harvest three seedpods: one for science at her institute, one for her personal collection and one for her cooking tonight at his home when she would keep her promise to prepare a Mexican meal. She eagerly complied, taking three seedpods, and then set her mobile in camera mode and began capturing images of the plants she had harvested. As Margarita circled the plants, stepping carefully among them and keeping her eyes and thoughts completely focused on recording images from every possible angle, suddenly Shema said firmly, "Quickly, back to the walkway."

He grabbed her elbow and pulled her inside, shoving the gate closed with

8

his foot. "Gee, Shema, was I getting too close?" Margarita said disappointedly.

"Not at all, we were in danger. I heard Bozo. He can be sneaky. And his sense of humor is very apelike. He would have tossed you over the walkway and then laughed until his belly shook."

"Bozo!" Margarita asked, "Who in the name of green mung beans is that!"

"Our eight-hundred-pound gorilla."

In 2030, animal management programs include practices that rotate managed animals through clones of their natural environments. It was well understood by the end of the second decade of the century that captive gorilla heart ailments were related to their lack of Grains of Paradise in their diets. As with many species, it was learned that introduction of native diets to animals worked most smoothly by rotating them through bioclone pods of their ancestors' habitats.

The decision was made to keep Bozo as a permanent resident of Shema's bioclone pod because he was helpful, and happier there than in the animal park in New York where he had been born and raised. He had arrived at the pod with the first batch of adolescent gorillas and had proven a natural leader and protector of the others. When the other eleven gorillas were rotated out after eighteen months, Bozo was kept on site to welcome the new eleven gorilla youngsters who arrived. He welcomed them enthusiastically and showed them the ropes. Bozo proved to be an ideal member of the bioclone pod team except for his one bad habit, tossing female human visitors.

When Shema explained Bozo's background to Margarita she narrowed her eyes and told him, "Bozo needs a wife."

Shema replied, "I'm not going there—at least not until after you show my wife how to cook tamales."

The Eight Hundred Pound Gorilla

An eight hundred pound gorilla is lifting kids today and tossing them into the future. He has got them by their pockets and is not about to let go. A high percentage of people in charge of children have tried to ignore the gorilla, or pretend he will go away. With every passing moment, the gorilla gets more conspicuous and the pretence that he will fade more awkward.

When this Bozo—this eight hundred pound gorilla who is altering forever the lives of the people who are now young—is noticed, he is referred to as the "mobile phone" or the "cell phone." Neither term is accurate any more. This gorilla is morphing at warp speed into much more than a phone. The most accurate term we have for the device he represents is simply the "mobile."

What makes the expression about the eight hundred pound gorilla so wonderful is that we have learned gorillas are not necessarily bad guys. Scary, yes. Powerful, oh my yes. For certain, they are something we need to notice when there is one in the room. But often they are very much worth preserving and nurturing into the future. That is what we should be doing with the mobile Bozo that has grasped kids by the pockets. The purpose of this book is to take a look at the principles in play that are creating the future the gorilla is waiting to tell us about.

I have found it easier to explain these principles by referring to examples of future people for whom they are operational in their lives than it is to hypothecate on and on about what could happen. Probably the most common trait in the new generation across the planet is that they will have a mobile device as they go through their youth and beyond. Their future is mobile. Using their mobile devices their generation will connect to what is known and to each other globally. That, by any measure, is a gorilla of the grandest dimensions.

The older siblings of children born in the 2000s are mobilists already. I do not have to prove that to you. Wherever you may live, you know that is true of teenagers and pre-teens. There are already places where nearly everyone, including the kids, has at least one mobile, including Japan, South Korea, Finland, Hong Kong, Norway and the UK. China and India's enormous markets are absorbing the devices ravenously. Young people in the United States are relentlessly acquiring mobiles. Even with all of that mobile ownership in the more technologically advanced countries, the largest number of subscribers to mobile services are in developing countries—and there the new generation is the vanguard.

In Tibet, every village including the most remote ones now has mobile service. In Peru and neighboring Latin American countries the telcons are at war to see which can supply mobiles most effectively to remote countrysides. The African miracle of mobile access seems certain to mean the process of installing wired desk computers will be leapfrogged over in many—perhaps most—places there. The Arab mobile market multiplies and multiplies. And so it goes around the world.

Today's teenagers and younger children not only have mobiles. They are very heavy users of the devices. They use them to talk to over the phone. They send text messages back and forth. They take pictures and listen to music. In developing countries they operate mobile phone booths selling call time to people on the streets. Around the world, more and more affluent students who can afford smart phones use them to access study knowledge from the Internet. Scattered, too, here and there are events when kids summon mobs for protest or fun using their mobiles for assembly.

The Washington Post published an article on October 14, 2006 gives some mobile flavor from India:

> At the beginning of 2000, India had 1.6 million cellphone subscribers; today there are 125 million -- three times the number of land lines in the country. With 6 million new cellphone subscribers each month, industry analysts predict that in four years nearly half of India's 1.1 billion people will be connected by cellphone.
>
> This explosive growth has meant greater access to markets, information about prices and new customers for tens of millions of Indian farmers and fishermen. A convenience taken for granted in wealthy nations, the cellphone is putting cash in the pockets of people for whom a dollar is a good day's wage. And it has made market-savvy entrepreneurs out of sheep herders, rickshaw drivers and even the acrobatic men who shinny up palm trees to harvest coconuts here in Kerala state.[1]

The Washington Post article featured fishing boat captains who work off the coast of the southern tip of India. While at sea, as they make their catches they are able to negotiate and sell them using their phones to talk with wholesale agents in port. Their profits are significantly increased by the timely information they can relay wirelessly.

One of the major planetary events of the first decade of the 21st century is the spread of mobile phones to cover populations worldwide. By mid-decade, nearly half of the 6.5 people on earth had a mobile phone. It is significant that this new technology broke out of the usual pattern for the spread of new technology. The surprise is that the majority of mobile phones were in developing countries by mid-decade, and that trend was strengthening.

In June 2006, I attended iSummit06 in Rio de Janeiro, where I was one of the bloggers for the conference. The iSummit was about the emerging cultural commons within the digital world. It was attended by representatives of fifty-five counties, both developed and developing. In his keynote for the conference famed musician Gilberto Gil, who held the post of Minister of Culture of Brazil, spoke to aspirations for people who have not before been connected. As I posted

[1] http://www.washingtonpost.com/wp-dyn/content/article/2006/10/14/AR2006101400342.html

on the event's blog:[2]

> Gilberto Gil described the vision of people now living in the 19th
> century leaping over the problems of the 20th century to enjoy an open
> world in the 21st. He spoke of possessing the attitude in his own heart
> of having been born by the sea. He offered this hope, inspired by his ad-
> monition of those from by the sea: Let their gaze be lost in the horizon.

That poetic view speaks to the jolting reality, that the horizon has jumped
into the hands of people in the Amazon jungles, the Andes Mountains, the
Asian steppes, the African bush, distant islands and hinterlands worldwide.

The mobiles that pour into developing countries are, for now, mostly handsets with voice and texting features. Still they are mobiles as the term is used in
these pages: a personal tool an individual carries for doing things interactively in
the new digital world. For many individuals in developing countries, acquiring
one of these voice and texting mobile handsets is to do quite literally as Gilberto
Gil hoped: leap from the 19th century, over the 20th century, into the 21st.
When historians look back, they will note that the overarching difference the
mobile in the form of a telephone made was that in the first decades of the 21st
century everybody on earth got one: phones were the first way virtually everyone
owned a mobile, using it to interact for the first time with the new digital world
that emerged as the 20th century wound down.

As this book goes to press only about one billion people use the Internet, yet
nearly half of the 6.5 billion people on earth have a mobile phone. The momentum seems to be in place so that essentially everyone on earth will have a mobile
that includes a phone within a few years. Put another way, one-by-one during
the next very few years countries—including the least developed in other ways—
will join those where the mobiles already outnumber the population.

Mid-decade mobiles with voice and texting features are closing the digital
divide, at least to the extent that they are connecting vast new populations into
the interactive digital venue. The mobile telephone is the first technology for
which the majority of users are located in developing countries, and that trend is
increasing. Wireless transmission is leapfrogging the need to unroll cable spools
across tech-empty distances. Instead, as the metaphor goes, circles of transmission are spreading like lily pads until they will overlap to cover the planet with
wireless availability.

The eight hundred pound gorilla is a global player. He is making the lives

---

2http://www.icommons.org/isummit/report.php?rID=87

of the new generation throughout the world very different than anything their parents could have imagined even such a short time ago as when their youngsters were born. Teenagers in developing countries have become at least as knowledgeable about mobiles as their contemporaries in the digitally privileged countries. Teenagers in Africa are running street businesses where they sell phone time to passersby. The littlest ones there may not be running the businesses yet but they are absorbing what their older brothers and sisters are up to with the thirsty brains of interested toddlers. South and Central America are experiencing cost cutting competition among mobile phone providers who are proving their merit by transmitting connection and flooding devices into remote locations. Today's youngest children in these far off places will not remember a time without mobile phones. The story is the same in mean streets and hinterlands of every country, as well as in the posh and pampered kids' rooms of the most connectivity advanced lands.

We cannot understand the future that will belong to the new generation without recognizing the mobile Bozo. Although Shema and Margarita are not specific real people, they exist. The technology wave in Rwanda is underway. Shema at age seven as this book is published has every chance to own mobile models as they advance, and to follow that sequence into the science of Africa's long treasured Grains of Paradise. Margarita, now a child of Shema's age in the Rio Grande Valley could easily find her way to schooling at the New Mexico Spaceport where construction is planned to begin in 2007.

Shema, Margarita and their contemporaries worldwide are already very much aware now of what for most older generations is still the proverbial eight hundred pound gorilla. Mobiles are a big part of their lives and plans, as the pages ahead explore.

Interactive

The One-Way Media Museum
July 2040

The dashboard map sights-to-see selections for Des Moines, Iowa flashed "The One-Way Media Museum." Charlie clicked the "Info" button and this museum message appeared:

> See action from the age before interaction: get beamed at, feel broadcast blasts, experience that bombarded sensation the old folks talk about. Be told what to think without being able to respond. Full range of print and on air media.

"Cool, as they would have said back then," Charlie proclaimed, "let's turn off here and take a look at that." Mildred obligingly guided their vehicle on to the off ramp, Charlie programmed the dashboard map to provide directions to the museum, and two teenage boys in the back seat groaned.

Within ten minutes Mildred had pulled on to the museum parking conveyor and the family was being carried to a vehicle space. The building holding the displays had once been a Dow Jones printing plant that had cranked out ink-on-paper copies of the Wall Street Journal. A large sign announced that original printing machines from the late 20th century were included in the one-way media displays.

When the family reached the main doors of the building the older boy walked rapidly at the doors, stumbling to get stopped before he hit the firmly shut glass panels. "The place must be closed," he mumbled. Then he noticed a sign on the door that said "PUSH." He touched it. The door did not move as a deep voice said, "Push hard, this door only interacts with human muscle." The boy pushed the door open and the rest of the family followed him into the lobby area of the museum.

Ahead of them near an interior door was a little house-like building with a man inside. He was looking at them through a window. Charlie walked over to the man and reached into his pocket for his mobile. The boys looked at their mother and asked her in unison, "What is Dad doing."

Mildred explained that the man was in what used to be called a ticket booth before interactive entry software made them obsolete. "It used to be a very boring job, sitting all day taking people's money and handing them paper tickets. I wonder how Dad is going to get us in if they don't use mobile cash."

Walking back, Charlie said, "Well, they are pre-interactive except for taking my money. The guy was happy to let me beam him my payment, but he did give me paper tickets."

"What do we do with those?" the older boy asked.

"They are just souvenirs." Charlie said. "They are not about to pay another salary for a real old time ticket taker. We can go straight on in."

As they wandered into the display room, the first group of exhibits were radios. The younger boy walked over to a 1940 radio console, pointed his pocket mobile at the machine and clicked the universal activation button. The same voice that had told his brother to push the door now boomed, in a slightly impatient tone: "Turn the big knob at the right." When the boy obeyed, the dial of the machine lighted up and a voice came out of the fabric-covered center of the radio. It was ranting in German.

"You are listening to Adolf Hitler," volunteered the hidden voice. "Radio is a one-way medium. You can turn Hitler on or off but you can't tell him what you think." That was all the voice said. The family of four stood there silently staring at the situation of a hundred years earlier, and listening to the rant whose words they could not understand."

The older boy said, "I am going to turn him off." He reached over and turned the knob until it clicked off.

The One-Way Media Museum had over a dozen television exhibits, covering the age of TV that characterized most of the second half of the 20th century. Each exhibit included a brief comment from the unseen voice.

The black and white television from the early 1950s played clips from the McCarthy Hearings. The 1960s featured hippy and drug news coverage. In the 1970s there were clips from the Watergate investigations and the 1980s showed the explosion of the Challenger Space Shuttle. The 1990s showed news coverage of President Clinton during the Monica Lewinsky investigation.

As the family sat at a table munching some snacks before moving on to the print section, the boys were full of questions. They wanted to know what else was going on when these big stories were on television. The fact that there had only been three networks in the United States during all of those years surprised them. Their realization that the three networks usually said about the same thing surprised them even more. "What if McCarthy was right, how would you find out?" asked the older boy. "Was Bill Clinton the only President who had a girlfriend?" the younger boy wondered.

Hearing Hitler had gotten the boys thinking even more. Their father explained to them that during the age of radio dictators could say whatever they wanted to and the people had to listen to them or listen to nothing. In free countries radio was a powerful one-way medium too. Winston Churchill and Franklin Delano Roosevelt used the radio to inform their citizens, and during times of crisis to say reassuring and calming words to the public. When the boys asked how the citizens could respond, Charlie said they could write letters and that was about it. There was no citizen medium. You could not interact directly using radio or television.

"People did protest rallies and stuff like that," Charlie explained. "In countries like Nazi German, though, you didn't protest at all. If you did, you got shot."

After their snack the family visited the printing exhibits. The boys saw the first printing machines without recycle slots that they had ever laid their eyes on. It seemed incredible to them that every day acres and acres brand new of paper had gone into the machines. The boys had both been born after 2020 when the last non-recycling machine had been taken out of service and melted down so the metal could be used for another purpose.

Mildred, Charlie and their sons ended their visit to the One-Way Media Museum in the room that exhibited early models of book recyclers. The museum allowed visitors to recycle a book if they brought an original book with them to use in the process. Mildred pulled a book out of her pack and offered to her sons. After a small amount of dissention, it was decided that the younger boy would drop the book into the hopper and the older boy would select which new book to have the machine make.

The older boy pointed his mobile at the recycler and started clicking keys. "This is more like it, he said. Now I am communicating with a machine that will take my orders." Without explaining what he was doing, he chose a book he knew was one of his mother's favorites, and picked a lavender color for the cover because he knew she liked that too. When he finished with the instructions to the machine, he told his brother to drop the old book into the hopper. As soon as he had done so, the machine began to make noises. An indicator said the process would take fourteen minutes.

The One-Way Media Gift Shop was just around the corner from the recycle machine. The family traipsed into it and began looking around. Mildred went straight to the books section while Charlie and the older son started looking at the replica reconstruction kits. The younger son quietly joined his mother. "Who was Hitler, he asked?"

"Well, I guess you could say the was Mr. One-Way Message of the 20th century. He was the dictator who led Germany in starting World War II." She went on to explain that the radio exhibit was an authentic reproduction of the way things actually were. "Hitler could say anything and people had no choice except to listen. He particularly went after young people like you. If we were living right now in Germany in 1940, you and your brother would be in the Hitler Youth organization and there would be nothing your father and I could do about it. The awful thing is you would probably be very pro-Hitler and would agree with whatever he said."

The boy thanked his mother and started clicking around in his mobile that he had pulled out of his pocket. He spoke to her again in a few minutes telling her he wanted to read a couple of things Hitler had said. She listened as he quoted: "He alone, who owns the youth, gains the future." "Make the lie big, make it simple, keep saying it, and eventually they will believe it."

Before Mildred could think of anything to say, Charlie and the older son showed up and said the time was up for the recycle machine to have finished. The four of them walked back to the machine and the older boy reached into the output bin. He handed his mother a freshly printed book with a lavender cover. She looked at the title page, gave him a hug and they started toward the museum exit.

The boys began arguing over whether the recycled books were more environmentally friendly than mobile books. By the mid-2030s, access to a mobile book was universal. For a large percentage of people the mobile book was no more than a feature for the mobile device they carried with them all the time. For others, a mobile book could be obtained for no cost.

The recycle machine and the mobile book developed in parallel during the first decades of the 21st century. To use the recycler, you simply dropped an old book in one end and a new printed one like Mildred got came out the other end. The recycler could be set for various sizes and weights of pages, fonts, color or black and white images and other specifications. Often it would take two old books to produce one new book; this was almost always true when the output book would be longer or higher print quality than the book or books being recycled.

The recyclers argued that their products were more comfortable to hold, and easier on the eyes to read because the printed books had reflected light instead of light reaching the eyes directly from its source. By internalizing the shredding, paper production, type-setting, printing and binding into a single-location machine, paper waste was almost eliminated and production costs were very low. When a book was created this way, the words and images were downloaded into the recycle machine from the Internet, making it possible to print almost any book in existence within a very few minutes.

The mobile books of 2040 were elegant little devices displaying pages that looked exactly like printed paper to the human eye. Any book that could be downloaded from the Internet for printing could also be downloaded to be displayed as a mobile book.

The very big difference between recycled books and mobile books was that the recycled books were one-way media and the mobile books were interactive. After Charlie and Mildred's family were back in their car and once again on the road rolling across Iowa, the younger boy sat quietly interacting with his mobile. Charlie was in the front seat where his older son was at the wheel.

Mildred sat next to her younger son. He turned to her after a lot of miles in which her nose was in the lavender book and his near his mobile. "Mom," he said. "The mobile books are better." She look pleased. Her expression was questioning. He explained that he had downloaded Adolf Hitler's book *Mein Kampf* and that he had been clicking through to read some of the annotations there, and looking at some other places about Hitler on the Internet. "What if I were a Hitler Youth listening to this back when Hitler was alive?" he whispered. "If I couldn't check it, I would believe everything he told us."

Mildred said, "That is right, exactly right. That is what happened. Interacting with Hitler was not possible. Ideas just moved one way: from him at his people."

Interaction

My earliest memories of media include one of the live voice of Hitler coming through the static of a short wave radio broadcast tuned into at my grandparents' home in Texas. More routine in the years when I was in early grade school during World War II was the broadcast voice of Kate Smith, soothing a national United States audience with her signature singing of "God Bless America." Listeners responded to these broadcasts only in our psyches. The messages were one-way: at us.

In 2007 at age nine, my grandniece is a regular watcher of American Idol, where she can interact with the television program by texting her vote for a contestant. The ability of millions of people to respond immediately to something coming to them through old-time one-way media is a remarkable contrast to the broadcast era that dominated the 20th century.

The leaking of interaction into traditional broadcast media is an overflow from the inherently interactive Internet. The Internet is not only two-way, it is omni-way. Omni means all: the Internet is a medium that can move information in all directions and whoever receives information can respond in any and every direction. The Internet is a medium of interaction.

At Christmastime 2006, I watched another of my grandnieces as she looked at educational DVDs broadcast from her grandparents' television. She quietly sat behind a tiny table in a small chair staring at the screen. Clearly she was absorbed by the material she watched, and she was eager to watch the same DVD over and over again.

Someone had also given her a toy that was a flat panel with many buttons and levers to push, each one of which responded with a different set of sounds and flashes of light and color. The panel was an interaction toy, in the sense that when a child pushed a button or pulled a lever the panel reacted. My grandniece played with the panel several times, and then seemed to lose interest. I assumed she had figured out how each of the buttons and levers would respond and then became bored.

Even at less than two-years-old, as this tiny girl was during Christmas 2006, she was able to reach the limitations of the toy that interacted with her. She was quick to ask again for the broadcast from the DVD which she could sit and watch passively. The DVDs that her parents had provided for her are the products of experts who create learning materials for children. The broadcasts are fun and informative, and one-way.

Nevertheless, her quick mastery of the buttons and levers on the toy showed that less than two years was old enough to interact by pushing and pulling. My grandniece was also, it looked like to me, plenty old enough to get frustrated by the same responses over and over. It is a mistake to think of the panel toy that bored her as interactive in the way her mobile future will be.

When they are older, the interaction that children her age will hold in there hands through mobile devices will be omni—in all directions. The device will interact with people, information, ideas, the business they do and with most of the projects they undertake. Even one-way material like the DVDs my grandniece watched will become interactive as they move primarily on to the Internet. The voting on *American Idol* is an example of that happening already.

It is fair to say that every webpage is a multiple invitation to interact. You can interact by choosing (or not choosing) to read items on the page and/or look at images. You are offered text, images and buttons to click—to cause the page to interact with you by providing new information, starting a video or by displaying a different page. The new page in turn is there to interact with you.

When my grandniece's parents decide it is time for her to interact with the Internet, they might sit with her as she opens the homepage of Disney.com, where dozens of options clamor for her interaction, a little like the buttons and levers do on the panel she briefly enjoyed and then got bored with in 2006. The parents might tell her to choose from *Playhouse, Games, Kids Island* and *Character Gallery*. Each of those choices would lead to more choices, and each of them to still more choices. On every webpage will be links to other clusters of choices both in Disney's children's materials and in other Disney and Internet locations. Instead of interactions that are dead ends like the panel had, each new choice opens many more new doors and interconnected pathways.

A great deal has been said that frightens parents about the astounding connective potential of the Internet. It is true that a child clicking around in a Disney game is only a few clicks away from pornography—a fact that has not and probably will not change for anyone visiting the open Internet. As a person of any age learns to interact with the Internet, clicking around in websites with raunchy pictures and language is an option.

The pornography red flag has been a major factor in limiting the interaction with the Internet by students at school. Educators have routinely selected what websites students can access and blocked others. They have modified use of the Internet at school from omni-connective to choices controlled by school authorities.

By the end of the first decade of the 21st century, schools will effectively lose their power to keep students from interacting with the open Internet. That will happen because the open Internet will soon be available on the mobile each student owns. For the past ten years most schools have presumed to regulate student use of the Internet by providing computers that are wired down in classrooms, with time allotted to individual kids. The connections of these computers have filtered out unapproved (by the schools) websites. This process has pushed the way the new generations has been allowed to use the Internet back toward one-way media, adding a boredom factor that even my under two-year-old grandniece experienced when her interactions with her toy panel led over and over to closed doors.

The control of use by students of computers occurs over the broad range of schools, including those in the developing world. In a January 2007 article about the One Laptop Per Child Project, its leader Nicholas Negroponte is quoted with this lament:

". . . one of the saddest but most common conditions in elementary school computer labs (when they exist in the developing world), is the children are being trained to use Word, Excel and PowerPoint," Mr. Negroponte said.

"I consider that criminal, because children should be making things, communicating, exploring, sharing, not running office automation tools."[1]

The threat of kids finding porn, encountering dangerous people online and/or using digital tools to cheat or take naughty pictures are the justifications educators give for controlling the interactions of students with the new virtual world known as the Internet—trying, as it were, to make the grand new interactive resource into a one-way medium controlled by the education establishment. As the mobile phones have threatened this control of their students, educational authorities have generally forbidden them to have the devices in school. Fortunately, denying youngsters access to their mobiles is having minimal effect on what those mobiles are becoming.

The personal and free interaction with the Internet that the mobile is beginning to put in a student's hand turns a powerful spotlight on just exactly how what that student is learning has been controlled at school for the past decade. The Internet is an open commons of knowledge where learners from across the world can study from the same page. It is a virtual place where individuals can connect in creative projects.

We were shocked in the mid-20th century, as Charlie and Mildred's boys were a hundred years later, by the way Hitler controlled what German youth were taught. Yet schooling has always involved choosing what students will be taught and testing them on whether they learned what was provided to them. Schooling has made learning into essentially a one-way medium, with testing and accrediting as a way of verifying that what was served up by educators was learned.

The mobile is about to provide a stunning option! That 800-pound gorilla is already bounding through the halls of schools worldwide, and sitting on playgrounds with kids in his lap, joyfully helping them understand how to use their little devices as an omni-way medium to communicate with each other and with the global online learning commons. He is teaching them to intertwingle.

In the mobile future, new generations will hold everything known by humankind in their hand—and will be able to interact with the stuff and help to

---

1BBC News. http://news.bbc.co.uk/1/hi/technology/6224183.stm?ls

refine and enrich it. That marvelous power of interaction with knowledge and with other learners is something completely new in human experience —a key factor coming to the new generation in their mobile future.

The Mobile

Doctor Celtel
October 2030

There was never a time Celtel could remember when his family did not talk about how wonderful two things are: newborn babies and mobile phones. He grew up sharing a deep appreciation for both. His mother reminded him often of how a mobile phone saved his life even before he was born.

The story he knew so well was that when his mother went into labor she was in their remote home village in Sierra Leone where there was no doctor or medical help of any kind. She managed to find one of the few mobile phones in the town and called his father who left work, borrowed a car, picked-up a midwife and arrived in time for his mother to be helped with his delivery. The grateful family named their newborn son "Celtel" after the telecommunications company that provided wireless connection to their village.

Celtel, born in 2006, has lived through great change in his native Africa. He acquired memories he could never forget of the suffering of children his age. He also saw and benefited from the massive progress that took place in Africa as he grew up. He decided at an early age that he wanted to become a doctor and to heal sick children. His parents and he persisted to get him past many obstacles as Celtel kept on a straight path to his goal.

By the compounded good luck of having a mobile summon assistance to his birth and being given his name, Celtel also got some attention from the telcon company whose name he bore. They saw to it that he had his own mobile throughout the years of his childhood, and after he proved on his own to be a star student, they gave him financial support for his advanced studies.

With a flavor of the old spiritual ways his grandmother would whisper to him when he was a small child, Celtel thought of the mobile as a serendipitous gift in his life. Along with his biological and medical studies, Celtel saw to it that he stayed fully trained and informed about mobiles. His medical school class-mates remember him as the fellow who devised holograms of anatomy specimens that could be conjured using their mobiles. As a student, he also worked on a mobile healing beam that showed promise for replacing bandaging of cuts with a quick mend of the severed tissue. That project earned him the nickname "Celtel McCoy" from the old Star Trek series.

With this rich mobile background, it surprised no one when Celtel began searching out and working on remote care for children. He was accepted in

2029, at age 23, for a residency at a children's hospital in Korea where work was being done on infant mobiles. The lead doctor of the program, Bae Kim, is known worldwide for his work in preventing SIDS, the Sudden Infant Death Syndrome that had been the leading cause of death at the beginning of the century in children one month to one year of age. The Mobile Monitor Bodysuit developed by Dr. Kim's group had proven effective in every case where it had been worn by a baby in which SIDS had occurred.

The field of remote medical monitoring was not new by the time Celtel reported to work in Bae Kim's program. Dr. Kim's office included a framed exhibit on his wall displaying his collection of antique monitors. One of the oldest, from the year 2002, had saved the life of his grandmother. The monitor was a simple two-way device worn around the neck. His grandmother, living alone in a small apartment in Seoul, had fallen and broken her hip. In her fall she had cut her arm badly and was loosing a great deal of blood. Unable to reach her landline telephone, she pressed the alarm button on the monitor hanging from a cord around her neck. The alarm signaled her son, Bae's father, and a nearby hospital. "And the rest is a history of a happy recovery," said Dr. Kim, as he finished telling the story to Celtel during their initial interview.

The two men were soon working very closely on their shared passion: making infants "unneglectable" as they liked call it. The challenge required perfecting three steps: output an infant's information to an online monitor; perfect the online monitor to recognize threats to the infant; output threat information to the infant's caregivers. Bae and Celtel worked almost exclusively on the first step. Their knowledge and training focused on the human body—especially the infant—equipping the doctors to invent and test ways to look for problems and transmit warnings.

The Sudden Infant Death Syndrome occurs when no one is aware that the infant has died. The Mobile Monitor Bodysuit Bae Kim had developed verified vital signs several times a minute and transmitted a warning if the signs were not there. Celtel envisioned accomplishing the same monitoring and warning using a small programmable patch, and Bae enthusiastically supported the idea.

The two men felt that if the patch could be small enough, cheap enough and sticky enough to stay put on an infant it would be possible for every newborn to wear one. By making it programmable, the patch could be customized for different parts of the world so it could alert caregivers to local diseases. They also planned to develop feedback programs to create ways for the patch to serve as a true mobile by sending instructions to the infant's system to restart breathing, adjust body temperature and otherwise protect and extend the child's life.

The second step for seeing to it that the world's infants are unneglectable is being worked on in 2030 by two main centers: the research division of the Babies Hospital of Bombay and the pharmaceutical behemoth Pillmountain Ltd. based in Switzerland. The competition between the two centers is considered healthy because it is keeping both groups focused on perfecting the warning applications they are developing to receive and evaluate digital warnings coming in from infant mobiles around the world.

The math for evaluating the warnings online is simple and awesome: one online application could evaluate every infant in the world at the same time and all the time. The savings in lives and medical costs makes the economics of such a system hugely profitable. By separating the evaluation of what is going on out of the limitations of the mobile patch, and putting it into the unlimited computer capacity of the online cloud, diagnostics could as be powerful and sophisticated as human ingenuity can contrive.

In the third step, a warning is sent to caregivers for the infant whose mobile has detected something that may be endangering the child. That warning can give an alarm through the personal mobile of each parent and other family and caregivers, and to local health facilities and police.

As Celtel, not yet thirty-years-old, looks into the future beyond his residency with Bae Kim, he expects the 2030s and 2040s will be the decades in which children's illnesses will be eradicated worldwide. He smiles remembering that his mother's quick thinking in finding one of the old mobile phones at the time of his birth was really the same principle that was now guiding his work and dreams. "Digital communication," he thought, "belongs in the list of history's great medical innovations, along with the germ theory of disease, anesthesia and vaccinations."

Mobile Morning

The name of the young doctor of the future described in this chapter's story is inspired by this MobileAfrica.net report of September 2006:

> A pregnant woman at home alone in her remote village in Sierra Leone unexpectedly went into a difficult labor and, with no access to a doctor or medical facilities, a minor medical emergency could have taken a tragic turn.
>
> But the woman, Emma Sesay, managed to use one of the few

cellphones in the village of Port Loko and called her husband, who borrowed a car and rushed home from his job, picking up a midwife along the way. They arrived in time to help Sesay give birth to a healthy boy, whom she promptly christened Celtel, the name of the cellphone company that provides services in her village and many others across 14 African countries, including Burkina Faso, Kenya, Uganda and Madagascar. [2]

The real Celtel is one-year-old as this book goes to press. I have no doubt that a Rwandan boy his age can be ready, willing, able to undertake the adventure just described. People Celtel's age, your age or my age, have never before had what the mobile will give to Celtel. We will have global participation in information and human affairs in our hands. This means knowledge and freedom that are ours individually.

Celtel's story takes place in the world of people too young to remember before the Internet era. The youngest of this new generation, like Celtel, are small children today. Soon they will be rambunctious youngsters, then awkward adolescents, and after that they will take their places doing the work of the world and pursuing their individual happiness. Much of that work will include important use of mobiles. Along with their right to the pursuit of happiness will be their new global civil right to the open commons within the global communications cloud.

The mobile is a device that before long will be carried and used by essentially each person on the planet as his or her personal tool. That tool will connect its owner into the billowing communications cloud enveloping Earth. The pages ahead will describe key factors about the mobile and the cloud, and will then take a look at what is about to happen when they integrate and fully energize each other—and do so on a global scale. Several aspects of the intertwingling that will result will be explored.

It is easy now to think of terrorism and the global economy as the two big things that will shape the 21st century. That view from within the first decade of the new millennium is a sour one—and one that I think is shortsighted. Two big things described in this book, the mobile and the cloud, form terrorism's obstacle and will form the platform of entirely new ways of conducting human affairs. The ubiquitous mobiles interacting with the global communications cloud will do many good things, none more important or wonderful than causing the emergence of the global knowledge commons in which we all learn

2http://www.mobileafrica.net/a75.htm 09.02.06

what is known by humankind from the same virtual page. At the least, light will be cast into the shadows where terror hatches, and productive competition will be encouraged. I would go much farther than that to say a global golden age is dawning, that an enlightenment is emerging in which terrorism can only shrivel and prosperity flourish.

To glimpse the course of a person's life in the mobile tomorrow, imagine that the cell phone you hold in your hand shrinks, flattens and becomes soft and sticky on one side. Think of placing it on to the tiny back of a newborn infant. From there it silently sends information to a center in the cloud where software nurses are constantly on alert to detect dangers the child's body may be experiencing as it adjusts to the world outside it's mother's womb. As something bad began to happen for the baby, alerts are sent to mobile devices of the parents and doctors. As the child grows, its uses of mobiles will change and diversify, capturing changing advantages of staying connected to the communications cloud.

The mobile is the individual person's tool for engaging the new virtual world. What we think of today as a mobile telephone will become a device first with many features, and then it will mature into an elegant tool for interacting with a panoply of functions of the Internet within the communications cloud.

In 2007, however, the mobile is a long way from being versatile, mature or elegant. The definition of a mobile is not clear in most people's minds. In first decade of the 21st century the mobile was born as a cranky, noisy little machine that at first could only interact with the wireless transmission clouds by sending and receiving voice and text messages. Nevertheless, this immature device was able to jump into billions of pockets—especially those of the younger generation.

New technology often strikes people as crude and disruptive. Making times of change even less comfortable, early adopters tend to act superior and to keep the rest of us in the dark about what is going on. New technology almost always requires that we give up comfortable habits and learn how to do whatever has gone obsolete in new ways. Adding insult to disruption, the new devices and methods almost always appear downright unfriendly in themselves. The new ones today tend to sport weird little lights blinking here and there and odd shaped buttons that have tiny, meaningless labels in dark gray lettering against the dull black color of the device.

Are you old enough to remember the arrival of the basis of today's mobile banking: the ATM machines? It was not pretty. An earlier form of remote of banking had been deposit by mail, in which you endorsed checks and mailed them in special envelopes that provided a deposit slip. That method required waiting for the envelope to be delivered, and then deposited by a human at the bank. To get our paychecks into our accounts faster, most of us did what our parents and grandparents had done. We spent part of every payday standing in a teller line inside of a bank building waiting to deposit our checks and to withdraw enough cash to last until the next time we were paid.

The first ATM machines that I remember were inside of banks, where they provided an option to the human teller line. When the machines began appearing in locations other than inside of banks incidents ranging from controlled frustration to open violence were common. For what seemed like a very long time, there was only one ATM machine at any remote location. Lines formed, and you waited. The machines were new and often would not perform. An entire genre of cartoons developed over reactions of people to ATMs that malfunctioned, refusing to give them their own money. I recall an instance reported in the newspapers where a man took a hammer to a recalcitrant machine and dented the senseless thing in several places. These problems were solved apparently by the same genius who thought of putting two rolls of tissue into restroom cubicles. The multi-machine ATM centers made things much better because if one was broken or being coped with by someone taking inordinate time, there was an alternative.

Another and far more serious ATM problem was that the machines attracted both criminals and people looking for a place to beg or to sleep. These aspects of the new mobility of banking were not humorous. A lot of people were robbed and some were hurt and even killed. Banks hired guards and stationed them where the machines were. Elaborate surveillance systems were designed and installed that made the ATM centers increasingly safe.

A mobile device that is the great-granddaddy of the iPod caused other kinds of public misery. Boombox owners would turn the machines up to full volume and then walk across a beach, park, or down a sidewalk. Here in New York City the boomboxes at full volume caused fights in subway cars where sound waves and combatants bounced off car walls. In 1979 Sony invented the Walkman—the first personal portable stereo—and the boombox brouhaha abated. Just as the iPod would do two decades later, the Walkman made it possible for a person to carry around his or her music while playing it privately through head phones. The iPod has added the power to interchange music to personal taste from the essentially limitless selection on the Internet.

There is no messier mobile arena than the one where the E-books have battled out device design, text formatting, and publication issues. Emotions are

30

triggered when the idea of an electronic book is floated at all. "I love books," we mutter, "don't mess with them!" The tech crowd are seen as enemies of the intellectuals. The comic relief is that it is the dirty-book readers who have been the biggest adopting group for E-books. After all, someone reading a handheld electronic display while riding in a commuter train is assumed to be doing office work, not reading a sexy book.

E-book designers are up against five centuries of craftsmanship in the printing field. Ever since Johannes Gutenberg printed his first unwieldy, ugly-lettered volume, work has been done to make reading a printed book easier and more pleasant. Printed books designed to be read by a human being sitting comfortably—curled up in a big chair on a rainy afternoon—are engineered to the last detail for that kind of reading. The weight is just right for the hands and lap, the feel of the paper is nice as the pages are turned, the color of the paper absorbs light that may annoy and reflects a crisp yet gentle image of words and phrases to the eye, the size and shape of the letters are ideal for the retina to grasp in gulps. Compare that experience to curling up with an electronic rectangle that beams light into your eye from behind letter shapes formed by pixels. Yet in spite of the visual challenges, E-Books are holding their own and getting better. In Japan it is popular on the commuter trains to read novels on tiny mobile phone screens. Go figure.

There are other mobiles that have become important quietly, not much noticed, as they have made changes in our lifestyle. An example of these is the Global Positioning System ("GPS"). The United States government put 27 satellites in orbit about 12,000 miles above the surface of the Earth. Solar powered, the satellites are routed in paths that carry each one around the Earth two times a day. The pattern of the orbit network places at least four satellites in view at any time from any point on Earth. A mobile GPS receiver is a device that can locate four of these satellites and then use trilateration (ask a geometry teacher) to tell you exactly where you are on the Earth's surface. The system is used in many ways. GPS information tells the computer in your car how to give you a route to your destination. GPS is available for children's mobiles making it possible for their location to be reported to parents and authorities. GPS tells wildlife scientists where the critters are on whom they have placed collars. And so on.

In the scheme of mobile things it would seem like a Personal Digital Assistant ("PDA") would be something everyone would want. Apple Computer, Inc. is well known for its spectacular successes with the Macintosh and other desktop computers and, more recently, with the mobile music iPod phenomenon. But Apple's PDA, the Newton, introduced in 1993, nosedived into oblivion in 1998. The big PDA success has been by Palm. In 2006, Palm's website *aboutPalm, Inc.*[3] page headlines: "Ten years. One vision. Palm celebrates 10-year Anniversary of the Pilot—the mobile computer that changed the way people work and live."

The wildly popular Palm Pilot of the late 1990s was a computer that you could carry in your pocket. This was new and exciting. The Palm Pilot's features were primarily what would replace pre-digital pocket items: an address book, a date book, an expense ledger, a memo pad, a to-do list, a calculator, and a digital age addition: e-mail. The Palm Pilot also had a very cool feature called Graffiti, that was a way to write by hand using a stylus. The first Palm Pilots were not wireless and interactive, but their descendents are. Palm's top-of-the-line in 2006 is the Treo—the mobile of choice for many discerning users. The Treo is a PDA, phone, Internet browser, and more. But we are getting ahead of our story. The original Palm Pilot was the quintessential PDA: personal. It was only mobile in the sense that it traveled with its owner. It was not wireless and could only interact with other computers through wires by syncing.

When the latest generations of the 20th century were children, handheld digital games flooded the toys market. I remember the early ones by Mattel, in the late 1970s, that my young nephews played endlessly in the car as the miles rolled by and their rambunctions were held in check. Each boy held a game between his hands. His thumbs moved rapidly and once in a while he would let out a whoop or a groan. In 1989 the introduction of Nintendo's Game Boy put handheld pocket computer games into the mainstream. In 2006 the PlayStation Portable ("PSP") sports the feature of the future: it browses the Internet. The PSP is a mobile that is already down the road toward the 21st century generations' world of tomorrow.

The October 11, 2006 the Online New York Times front page center picture showed the faces of five children crowding the screen of an OLPC. The headline read, "Laptops for All Libyan Schoolchildren." Under the picture the text said, "Libya reached an agreement with One Laptop Per Child, an American group developing an inexpensive, educational computer, with the goal of supplying machines to 1.2 million Libyan children by June of 2008." . . . "It is possible, Mr. Negroponte said, that Libya will become the first nation in the world where all school-age children are connected to the Internet through educational computers. "The U.S. and Singapore are not even close," he said."[4]

3http://www.palm.com/us/company/
4http://www.nytimes.com/2006/10/11/world/africa/11laptop.html?hp&ex=1160625600&e

Laptop computers are today's most obvious mobiles. Starbucks are filled by coffee sippers with their heads directed into the squared-off clamshell machines. Coveys of conference attendees move between sessions with their laptops held open. When television cameras sweep the scenes of government conferences the officials stretch their faces above their open laptops for photo ops. Once an airplane is in flight, the laptops are dragged to the trays in front of seats. The laptop is fundamentally the best effort so far to figure out how a person can take along his or her desktop computer without taking along the desk. One day before too long, the laptop we have now is going to seem as clumsy and out-of-date as the old square televisions have become when compared to the flat screen TVs.

Meanwhile, the device that is the most widespread mobile of the early 2000s —what the Americans call a cell phone and most of the rest of the world calls a mobile—is going through a rough patch of public annoyance like the early ATM and the boombox did. You have probably seen the following sort of scene that illustrates the less than perfect mobile image.

In September of 2006, I was riding a bus in New York City, traveling down Fifth Avenue along the edge of Central Park. The bus I was in was one of the hybrid models in which the electric motor compartment elevates the rows of seats at the back. I was in the second row of the elevated seats with an excellent view of the seating at the front of the bus. A passenger in a wheelchair was seated near the front door on the left side of the bus. He was a well-dressed man who appeared to be in his thirties. His wheelchair was a light weight athletic type, and he looked to be permanently disabled but not slowed down by his physical challenges.

Loud voices suddenly grabbed the attention of everyone on the bus. Sitting next to a window in a two-person seat opposite the man in the wheelchair was a woman who looked to be about the same age as the man. She was waving her phone at him and shouting, "I can talk as loud as I want to talk." He told her in a much quieter voice, but still audible to throughout the bus, that she was bothering everyone. She yelled some more at him and then went back to talking into the phone at the top of her voice. The exchange was repeated several times as the bus moved along toward Midtown.

As the verbal battle simmered and raged, the woman sitting beside me turned to me and said that she had gotten a cell phone only because her husband might need to reach her when she was not home. She told me smugly that it had only rung once—making me think her husband was taking some flak for insisting that she carry the phone. At that point the woman sitting in front of us turned around to tell us with that she had no cell phone at all. She, too, seemed quite pleased with herself. The two of them brought back memories of the early ATM days when a lot of people prided themselves in avoiding the untrustworthy machines as inappropriate technical intrusions into the gentle traditions of personal banking service.

These were well dressed women, and I would guess New Yorkers. Clearly they knew a thing or two—or at the least, like all of us New Yorkers, thought they did. Both of them were evidently very dubious about mobiles. When I proceeded to mention that I was writing a book about the young generation's future with mobiles, the woman sitting next to me looked me squarely in the eye and said, "Kids cheat at school when they have them!" The woman in front of us nodded knowingly. What went through my mind was a very popular expression we might have heard a century earlier right in the same spot on Fifth Avenue. If a rattling, exhaust-spewing new-fangled automobile rolled by, someone was likely to yell at the driver: "Get a horse!"

The world's kids today who have the marvelous new devices that had our bus crowd stirred up are living in the mobile morning. It is a time of the dawning of a new virtual world that already complements and enriches much of human experience. The youngest generation experiences the mobile morning in ways that those of us tempered by the 20th century have difficulty understanding. John Lienhard, writing in his book Echoes of Old Voices in the Rise of New Machines, tells us why the kids can see the morning better than we can:

> So with Menocchio in mind, let us look about us once more at over a billion computers that have been thrown into the world during a scant two decades. Like Sebastian Brant, we tell one another, "Gee whiz, look at all the information our children can now access". The real changes that the computer is bringing about – changes in the way we see reality – remain invisible.
>
> We hardly yet have an adult generation that has known the personal computer from birth. At this writing, you and I still see the computer against the backdrop of the not-computer. We typed before we word-processed. We learned the algorithms of arithmetic before we used hand calculators. We memorised facts, algorithms, and spellings.
>
> All of us see the personal computer against the backdrop of a world without it. What we cannot see at all is how a mind will work when it has never known anything else. What did they say about books in

1501? In the end, whatever was said was irrelevant because it was – ipso facto – useless commentary. For everyone looking at the new books in 1501, the future was as hopelessly unpredictable as it remains today. [5]

Those of us who can remember times before the Internet era—we who see mobile phones against the backdrop of a world without them—need to be careful before we condemn the devices and prohibit the new generation to use them. At the least, we should not harbor thoughts of putting the devices in a pile and burning them, as happened frequently after Gutenberg thrust books upon the people of his time.

There is something to be said for Lienhard's assumption that older generations "don't get it." An example of people like that are the Mayor of New York who brags about owning two iPods and then forbids students to carry them at school. As does the mayor, the two women on the bus who told me kids will cheat if they carry the phones use the devices to dismiss young people in a very cynical way.

It is difficult to excuse people who are responsible for youngsters for being dismissive. Actually, we are all responsible for the upcoming generation. The insight that Lienhard offers us is important in handling that responsibility. We who are older need to realize that the kids see and use mobile devices with a perspective that is ingrained in them and not in us. The early printers were not born into a world of movable type. They invented that world.

The generation that is now young did not invent mobiles: their parents and grandparents did. The kids, however, never knew a time when the mobiles were unavailable. Their minds are forming with the devices in their hands. People older than they are need to ask them what that is like—to learn from them. People of all generations also need to be willing to envision a changed future.

In writing this book, I have attempted to shed some light on mobiles from the perspective of the generation for whom they are native by imagining how mobiles will be used when the first of the new generation are in their thirties. One of the major ways in which these future mobile devices will be fundamentally different from today's mobile phones is that the features they provide their owners will be located not in the devices but in the global digital cloud emerging from the Internet.

The mobile device itself will be a tool of interaction with the connectivity

5Derek's Blog, http://blog.core-ed.net/derek/2006/11/the_end_of_education.html Quoting: Lienhard, John H. How Invention Begins: Echoes of Old Voices in the Rise of New Machines. Oxford University Press, 2006, p. 171

and content of the cloud. If you take pictures with your mobile the megabytes representing the images will transmit wirelessly directly into online storage. You will no longer need memory chips to insert into your mobile. If you are an infant and your mobile is measuring your heartbeat, your cardio record will be fed live into an online application that monitors and records it, and which incorporates your life information into a global commons of medical knowledge that profoundly informs medical science. If your doctor wants to look at your cardio record his mobile will respond to his click by projecting an image of it on to the wall or a holoscreen, as *Star Trek* could have called it, in the air.

The bottom line definition of a mobile is simple: it is a personal, portable, wireless device by which its owner interacts with the global virtual cloud into which the Internet is morphing. The next chapter takes a look at the cloud.

THE NEW PLACE
The major elements of the virtual world of digital connectivity

The Cloud

A Warming Friendship at Mount Erebus Antarctica
April 2030

Aada is a winter person, tempered by her childhood in Finland. Hot weather makes her feel closed-in. The most important factor in her preference for the Mount Erebus Resort is that the place is the coldest holiday farm in Antarctica, and that the coldest resorts in the world are now located on the South Pole continent.

Running a close second, and vying recently for number one factor in favor of Mount Erebus, is her warming relationship with Arturo. They had sipped wine together at the Watching Party on March 22nd, as the sun slipped behind the earth for the final time until the autumn equinox. She was looking forward to the possibility of a romantic summertime, and at age thirty, was permitting herself to hope quietly that marriage might even be a possibility.

Aada and Arturo have important, but very different, jobs at the resort. She is recreation director with the senior responsibility for seeing to it that the 800 paying guests enjoy themselves. Arturo is chief of temperature engineering, a job that can be summarized as seeing to it that the 250,000 servers under the resort are comfortable.

Mount Erebus Resort is one of the several dozen server farms located in Antarctic from where they provide most of the world's computing power. As the crisis deepened in the early 2010s, and more than half of the world's electricity had become necessary to cool the computers that provided global interconnectivity, the problem was solved by moving the heat-hog servers to the coldest place on earth. By 2030, the temperature and energy balance that had been achieved in the southmost continent was a success and a marvel.

In 2015, when the first Antarctic server farm was in the experimental stage, Arturo was looking for an engineering apprenticeship. Perhaps Arturo's DNA carried the engineering gift of his Inca ancestors, and probably the variety of climates in his native Peru helped his interest in environmental management. He had watched a video on his mobile that explained the plans for an Antarctic farm and offered the call for apprentice applications. Arturo went after a position and was given a slot.

Through the fifteen years since the then fifteen-year-old Arturo landed his apprenticeship, his learning and working lives were centered in the project. At first he continued attending a community center in his Peruvian village home.

The center featured applied arts, sports and social activities. Arturo excelled in the center's drawing program and won a national award for technical drawing.

The majority Arturo's learning life was conducted through his mobile computer, with guidance from his mentors at the server farm project where he apprenticed. He accessed subjects online and took tests that stepped him through the certification of his competency in math, physics, chemistry, environmental sciences, literature and languages. His apprenticeship included two stints each year working on site at the developing the server farm. His first trip to Antarctic was in 2021, when he spent only a summer. By 2025, Arturo was working full time on the project, spending alternate winters and summers at what had come to be called Mount Erebus server farm.

Aaba and Arturo were born the same year, in 2000. She was the youngest of four children and the only girl. The children's father was a Nokia executive and their mother operated a tourist center. The family lived in Espoo, Finland and was very much in the swing of the advanced technology—and in particular mobile—culture of the area. Aaba's brothers doted on their baby sister, providing her with tech toys from their large collection. She loved the attention and willingly communicated with the boys through whatever mobile device they had most recently equipped her with. Proud of his offsprings' enthusiasm for his line of work, their father kept them supplied with the latest devices coming out of Nokia.

But the times Aaba treasured were when she tagged along as her mother showed visitors around Finland. When Aaba was ten-years-old she got her oldest brother to make a special map for her to keep among her virtual tools. The map let her mark each new country and town for visitors she met on her outings with her mother. As she grew into her teens she began to add the email addresses of willing visitors whom she met on the tours—and soon was corresponding with people across the planet.

The family was not surprised when Aaba insisted that instead of a technology career, she wanted to train in the hospitality industry. She made that decision at the age of nine after spending a February day at her mother's office when the weather had become particularly fierce. Stranded tourists had been in and out throughout the day, seeking her mother's help. Aaba had enjoyed talking with a number of them, and had even found herself making suggestions to them about how to spend their time as the blizzard trapped them in the Helsinki area.

By age eleven, Aaba had her plans formed in detail. Her goal for her early teens was to earn certification in most basic school subjects online. To parallel that formal learning, she pestered her mother until an position was established for Aaba as a tourist agent apprentice, working through her mother's business. She also began a long range campaign to be accepted at the Cornell Hotel School, and was successful.

She spent the last four years of her teens in Ithaca, New York as an undergraduate student in the Cornell University School of Hotel Administration majoring in guest communications. Her major was a new field that was in hot development. Its underlying concept, which was to become basic to all hospitality fields, was mobile-based guest hospitality.

The core of mobile hospitality management is a customized program beamed into each guest's mobile upon arrive at a host facility. Access to and adjustment of amenities, directions, services, security, entertainment, billing and other hospitality matters are carried by the guest throughout a stay at the facility. Competition is, of course, genteelly intense among hotels, resorts, restaurants and spas for the most pleasure and satisfaction they can devise to implant in their guests' mobiles.

Mobile hospitality was born around the turn of the century when room keys began to be replaced by programmable plastic cards. Toward the end of the first decade of the new century, the smart cards had morphed into small mobiles with texting and Bluetooth beaming that could not only unlock a guest's door, but could control in-room electronics, send room service orders and reserve spa appointments.

By the time Aaba was at the Hotel School, personal mobiles had become as common as wristwatches and most travelers preferred to have hospitality management provided through their own mobile devices. Also by that time, the programming for hospitality management—like almost all common services programming—took place not in mobile devices, but in the Internet cloud. All that a guest needed to use hospitality management was a personal mobile that could interact with the Internet and a locator code to tell the mobile where to look on the Internet for the package personally customized for that guest.

Aaba found that what she had learned from her brothers and father helped her in her major, but her first love remained dealing with people. Her genuine affection and concern made her invaluable to the hotels and resorts where she began her career after her training at Cornell. It also supplied Aaba with a hilarious repertoire of stories about panicked and/or infuriated guests whom she was sent to assuage as they were locked in combat with their unresponsive mobiles.

Now in its third season, Mount Erebus Resort where Aaba and Arturo will spend the winter of 2030 is among the oldest of the Antarctic server farm

41

resorts. It was developed as and adjunct to a server farm first opened in 2013.

Antarctica server farms is one of those simple ideas—like the barcode or stuttering car window washer—that everyone wonders why they did not think of sooner. The problem moving the farms to the South Pole solved was not difficult to understand: the more computing the world demanded the more servers had to be running; running servers creates a lot of heat; cooling the servers takes a lot of energy. By 2010, over half the energy being produced on the planet was being used to cool down computers. Then somebody said: Why not place the process into an environment where the heat disappears on its own, instead of paying to cool the servers down? Why not Antarctica?

A typical Antarctic server farm is about ten square acres in size and built like a layer cake. The lowest layer is synthetic cold-transmitting plastic poured directly on to the ice surface and made level by reinforcing rods, creating a floor on the top. The next layer is a space with a twelve-foot ceiling supported by periodic pillars. The acres of servers sit on the cold floor of this giant room. The ceiling of the room is a thick, strong heat-absorbent layer that lifts the heat away from the servers. Arturo, as a temperature engineer, deals with balancing the cold from the floor, the heat from the computers, the heat absorbency of the ceiling and air circulation from the outside and within the space where the servers are—all to maintain an ideal temperature for the operation of the servers.

In the early building stages of the first farms, it was proven that the heat in the ceiling was an efficient way of melting ice that would run water-driven generators to provide energy to operate the servers. Captured heat is also used to insulate cables connecting the many Antarctic server farms and the five giant under-ice cable conduits that carry the information from the server farms to the Antarctic continental coast, where cables connect to the giant under sea cable to each of the other continents.

By 2025, the Antarctic server farms were providing over 80% of the world's computing. Studies indicated that global warming was deterred by the new location of the vast server farms for two reasons. They vastly reduced the amount of energy that had to be created to run the world's servers, and they eliminated server farm hot spots that had been scattered around the warmer continents.

Resorts like the one at Mount Erebus were not in the original planning of the server farms. They are pure serendipity. Once they were built, people began to realize that a server farm created a ten-acre, flat, warm surface—and that tempted human ingenuity. Most of the Antarctic science stations relocated on top of server farms to take advantage of the warmth, and the flat surface that can be used for airstrips. Other server farms have agricultural stations where the six months of sun and the underneath warmth are being studied for different food production scenarios.

The Mount Erebus Resort is a five-acre transparent bubble containing guest cottages, restaurants, spas, a nine-hole golf course, tennis courts and an elaborate amateur astronomy pavilion. During the Antarctic summer, guests can come for as little as two-weeks or as long as the entire summer. Winter stays are for the full six months because getting in and out of the continent in the worst winter weather still defies transportation technology. Winter visitors tend to include large numbers of astronomers who take advantage of the 24-hour viewing when the weather does not create cloud cover.

Arturo belongs to the second Mount Erebus community made up of the people who manage and operate the server farm. Although their working areas are beneath the top surface, they also have a bubble enclosure on top for residence and recreation. During the last days of sun in March of 2030, Aaba and Arturo frequently kept in mobile touch between their respective bubbles, texting back and forth and now and then popping up a halogram to share a laugh. Both of them were thinking to themselves that as the winter deepened, the two of them would add some extra warmth to what the server farm would generate that season. They each had unlimited privileges to use the under surface passageway between the farm and resort bubbles.

The Cloud

There is only one main theme of the story of Aaba and Arturo that is fanciful. Everything else is already well on the way to becoming reality. The giant server farms are already being built. The projection is real that says within a decade cooling down the machines that create our computing will require a majority of the power we can generate on our planet. The idea of locating the server farms in Antarctica is a futurist prediction of mine—with no other basis than my imagination. Who knows, though, maybe it has some merit.

The planetary computing cloud that will be central to the lives of people who are now kids traces its origins to the first distance communications. In 1900, the telephone was catching on. Poles were being setup along streets and roads. Wires were strung between the poles. In the beginning, the wires were all connected to a town's central switching board somewhere and extended out to individual businesses and homes. At the start of the 20th century telegraph wires had already been strung pole-to-pole between many towns around the world and across many countries. By 1900 six telegraph cables had been laid under the Atlantic Ocean, but none had yet been put in place under the Pacific Ocean. It would not be long before radio waves would be moving messages through the air. These would be one-way broadcasts mostly, but two-way radio was to become important later on.In the second half of the 20th century, the digital age developed and communications multiplied and diversified connectivity again and again. George Gilder painted a picture of the resulting tangle in October 1999, one year before the date our friends from the future Aaba and Arturo were born:

> Imagine gazing at the web from far in space. To you, peering through your spectroscope, mapping the mazes of electromagnetism in its path, the Web appears as a global efflorescence, a resonant sphere of light. It is the physical phase space of the telecosm, the radiant chrysalis from which will
> spring a new global economy.
> The luminous ball reflects Maxwell's rainbow, with each arc of light bearing a signatory wavelength. As the mass of the traffic flows through fiber-optic trunks, it glows infrared, with the network backbones looming as focused beams of 1550-nanometer radiance running across continents and under the seas. As more and more people use wireless means to access the Net, this infrared ball grows a penumbra of micro-waves, suffused with billions of moving sparks from multimegahertz teleputers or digital cellular phones. Piercing through the penumbra are rich spikes of radio frequencies confined in the coaxial cables circling through neighborhoods and hooking to each household. Spangling the Net are more than 100 million nodes of concentrated standing waves, each an Internet host, a computer with a microprocessor running at a microwave frequency from the hundreds of megahertz to the gigahertz. The radiance reaches upward between 400 and 800 miles to thousands of low-orbit satellites, each sending forth cords of "light" between Earth and sky in the Ku band between 12 and 18 gigahertz.[1]

In the last days of the 20th century, as Gilder captured so beautifully, we were still thinking in terms of a tangle of connections, from one point to another. But what was going on in the tangle was a great deal more than that. Intertwingling was underway, as the chapters ahead address. In this chapter we focus on the fundamental fact that the worldwide tangle of communications

---

1   Gilder, George. Forbes ASAP, October 1, 1999.

connections turned into a single global cloud.

By 2000, the number of connections available between points on our planet was incomprehensibly large, and growing faster and faster. For years, at almost every moment in time uncountable connections were added. The connections thickened every time a new computer was plugged in somewhere. More complexity was caused as webmasters spent their days connecting links to web pages and web pages to other web pages. Cable guys connected and connected as they worked shift after shift attaching more cables to more splitters and more boxes. Zillions of new static connections were hooked up continually to be in place when someone wanted to use them to interact with the online world.

The static connections are just half of the picture. Dynamic connections formed ongoing activity of billions of people every moment of every day. Whenever anyone talked on a mobile phone the connection was dynamic—happening in time and just for the duration of the call. Any time someone looked at a webpage and or moved among web pages the connections made were dynamic. Dynamic means the connections are made as you use them and gone when you stop. It wobbles the imagination to wonder how many human to digital dynamic connections are happening at any moment across the world. The number will multiply many times before the future year of 2030 in which Aaba and Arturo are falling in love during an Antarctic winter.

Behind all of the connectivity—static and dynamic—is human thought. Always, directly or remotely, the meaning of content of what is traveling over a connection has directed the linking. Computers are plugged in so they can be used by people or serve things people are doing. You make your phone call to exchange thoughts with another human. A third grade class that has made a webpage about butterflies links it to the Smithsonian butterfly page because the kids mean to have more butterfly content. The Smithsonian webpage about butterflies links to other insect pages because of the meaning of the content of each of the pages.

As tidy as that sounds, the online world is very messy as well. The growing density of the connectivity and the fact that using it got cheaper and cheaper began to allow junk to pile up. In the junk, the meaning behind the materials gets more and more remote. When the third graders moved on to the fourth grade no one remembered to take their butterfly webpage offline. The butterfly webpage put online by our third grade example is one of multiple billions of human projects that were anchored by an address in the open online world by the time Gilder was writing about the telecosm.

As the year 2000 brought a new century and new millennium, much of the enthusiasm for the Internet began its collapse into the DotBomb. While the touting and extravaganza of the 1990s were being blown up and away, the communications connectivity did not slow its expansion. Digital cynics snickered while, barely noticed, cables and beams multiplied.

A new sort of connectivity crept in and then took off. Towers and satellites spewed swipes of wireless connectivity across geography. By 2006, eighty percent of people on the planet lived in places where some wireless phone connectivity was available. As browsing the Internet becomes broadly possible through mobile phone devices, that percentage will begin to apply to online access. Direct Internet access began popping up in hot spots and spreading like lily pads across urban and then rural districts.

As 2006 moved toward its close, a resurgent digital world was beginning to be noticed. When an article about the future by George Gilder showed up in the October 2006 *WIRED Magazine* it created a bit of a buzz on the Internet: Gilder is back!

George Gilder's article was titled "The Information Factories" and the subhead read: "The desktop is dead. Welcome to the Internet cloud, where massive facilities across the globe will store all the data you'll ever use. George Gilder on the dawning of the petabyte age."[2] Here is Gilder's description from the article of the sizes we have and can anticipate:

> One characteristic of this new machine is clear. It arises from a world measured in the prefix giga, but its operating environment is the petascale. We're all petaphiles now, plugged into a world of petabytes, petaops, petaflops. Mouthing the prefix peta (signifying numbers of the magnitude 10 to the 15th power, a million billion) and the Latin verb petere (to search), we are doubly petacentric in our peregrinations through the hypertrophic network cloud.
>
> Just last century – you remember it well, across the chasm of the crash – the PC was king. The mainframe was deposed and deceased. The desktop was the data center. [Google founders] Larry Page and Sergey Brin were nonprofit googoos babbling about searching their 150-gigabyte index of the Internet. When I wanted to electrify crowds with my uncanny sense of futurity, I would talk terascale (10 to the 12th power), describing a Web with an unimaginably enormous total of 15 terabytes of content.

---

2   WIRED. October 2006, Issue 14.10. /www.wired.com/wired/archive/14.10/cloudware.html

Yawn. Today Google rules a total database of hundreds of petabytes, swelled every 24 hours by terabytes of Gmails, MySpace pages, and dancing-doggy videos – a relentless march of daily deltas, each larger than the whole Web of a decade ago. To make sense of it all, Page and Brin – with Microsoft, Yahoo, and Barry "QVC" Diller's Ask.com hot on their heels – are frantically taking the computer-on-a-chip and multiplying it, in massively parallel arrays, into a computer-on-a-planet.

In 1999, Gilder was describing connections among zillions of computers. In 2006, Gilder is describing the computer-on-a-planet that is called the cloud.

The communications that have engulfed the globe in the past decade might seem to be nothing more than new sorts of functional devices like those for sending of the telegraph message multiplied by an unimaginable volume and complexity. In fact, there is a big difference. In the cloud that is taking shape, a message launched from one point in the interconnections can be received by any or all of the other points and can do so essentially at the same time. In the open portions of the cloud, every point and every idea can be in touch with every other point and idea—in very close to real time! Things do not connect, they intertwingle.

The fact that communications work like a cloud seems perfectly obvious to a seven-year-old in 2007. To someone even ten years older, it takes some work to understand that the kind of connections they know of inside a desktop computer are now going on globally. For people of middle age and beyond the idea of a planetary computer that is a cloud can quite naturally strike us as absurd or mysterious. For younger people, the cloud is the way things are. The rest of us realize through our direct experience the coming of the cloud—an event that is among the handful or grandest changes in all of human history.

How the cloud functions can be seen in the future world of Aaba and Arturo: the many thousands of computers that form the Antarctic server farms are interconnected so that they can work as one computing machine. Computers in other parts of their 2030 world are also part of the one global cloud of digital power that serves the world population.

By the turn of the new millennium, the cloud was forming into a planetary computer. Within it, in an open commons, humankind—each person on the planet—will share one digital environment in which we can all participate, interact, contribute and learn. The biggest global gain from the cloud is that since the cloud is all one big interconnected computer, anything and anyone within it can intertwingle!

In the next chapter we look at the content inhabiting the Internet within the cloud.

Content in the Cloud

Omar O'Malley's Ospherology Orientation
September 10, 2035

The following is a portion of the transcript of the 25th annual Ospherology Orientation given by Dr. Omar O'Malley on September 10, 2035. A few notes of explanation have been inserted. Dr. O'Malley is referred to below as "Dr. OO," [phon. "oh, oh"] as he is known to all—including, some say, his wife.

NOTE: This much anticipated yearly webinar introduction to and update of the important 21st century science that studies online ospheres is logged onto by thousands of professional and amateur ospherologists. A few key leaders in the field are given query access privileging them to pose questions to the famous Dr. OO during his live presentation.

During the 13th webinar, in 2021, two of the questions posed led to some unseemly digressions, in the judgment of Dr OO. It was obvious to everyone that the digressions had gotten Dr. OO's Irish up. Deeply annoyed, the renowned osphere expert insisted thereafter on having the choice of answering or ignoring the questions by the inquirers.

Those with questioning privileges would, under the rules used thereafter, type a question which would then appear in small banner at the bottom of the viewers' screens. Dr. OO could then delete the question by clicking a button on his lectern, or respond to it by switching from his prepared remarks to discuss what the questioner had asked. Five minutes after a question was displayed, it would disappear from the banner if Dr. OO simply ignored it. A new tradition developed of secret betting pools in ospherologist circles to guess how many questions Dr. OO would delete, ignore or actually address. The most questions he had ever responded to during one of annual 2-hour events was four.

Dr. OO: The correct phonetic pronunciation of osphere is *oh spear*. It rhymes with *oh dear*. The emphasis is on the "o." The primary meaning of osphere refers to the overall knowledge contents of the virtual cloud that began to surround the earth just before the beginning of the 21st century. We badly needed a better word for content back then because the vocabulary got pretty confusing in the early 21st century.

I remember when I was in high school in the 1990s, words just showed up seemingly out of nowhere. The Internet was suddenly there and growing like a wild child. Words and phrases were used very loosely: information highway, surf, net, web, spider. One word that was exceptionally confusing was content. I remember wondering as a young teenager whether when the programming teacher talked about content if she meant someone was happy. Pretty soon, like all my fellow nerd geeks of the 90s, I used the word content to mean the stuff the digital networks were moving around.

NOTE: Omar O'Malley was born in Ireland in 1971. His mother was first generation Irish of Morrocan descent. His father's ancestry extends for centuries back into the Celtic mists of the green island. His nerd friends in high school in Dublin called him Druid, a name he secretly prefers. His wife calls him Druid, to good effect, on romantic occasions.

Dr. OO: The term osphere was first used in 2009, and as you may know I coined the word to get things clarified about content. Since the word cloud was already in common use to describe the massive communications connectivity that engulfed our globe like a great big nimbus, it seemed natural to turn to meteorology for some parallel vocabulary. Why not use an idea from the study of the physical atmosphere to give labels to the contents of the global cloud?

You see, there it is already! Atm-osphere. In Latin *atmo* means vapor, coming from *atm* that means something like blowing in Greek. Including the sphere part is important because putting atmo in front of it gives us a word that means a vapor that is "enveloping a heavenly body."[3] Meteorologists had used the osphere ending to built vocabulary for their sciences with words that meant different places and things engulfing our heavenly body the earth: exosphere, thermosphere, mesosphere, stratosphere, troposphere, ionosphere. Other earth sciences got into the act, as the Wikipedians have explained.

NOTE: A split screen appeared with Dr. OO on the left and these words on the right.

From the broadest geophysiological point of view, the biosphere is the global ecological system integrating all living beings and their relationships, including their interaction with the elements of the lithosphere (rocks), hydrosphere (water), and atmosphere (air).

---

3   Merriam-Webster Unabridged. http://unabridged.merriam-webster.com/cgi-bin/unabridged?va=atmosphere&x=47&y=12

Dr. OO: There was a new word that added the needed element for my idea to reach critical mass: in 2002, a blogger named William T. Quick suggested blogosphere. His idea was not related to the cloud, or meteorology or other earth science. Of all things, he got the word from philosophy! On January 2, 2002, Quick wrote on his blog the Daily Pundit the proposal to my right.

NOTE: The following text displayed on the right side of the split screen for one minute:

> I PROPOSE A NAME for the intellectual cyberspace we bloggers occupy: the Blogosphere. Simple enough; the root word is logos, from the Greek meaning, variously: In pre-Socratic philosophy, the principle governing the cosmos, the source of this principle, or human reasoning about the cosmos; Among the Sophists, the topics of rational argument or the arguments themselves. (The American Heritage® Dictionary of the English Language)[4]

Dr. OO: The idea, of course was mine, of applying the suffix osphere to the many divisions of human knowledge content within the Internet. In one fell swoop I caused the science of osphereology to come into existence. Comparing it to how Quick explained blogosphere is good way to show what an osphere is not. An osphere is definitely *not* a piece of cyberspace. An osphere is made up first and foremost of content. An osphere is not the space the content is in.

When I was growing up with the Internet—back in the 1990s and 2000s—an incredible amount of stuff was moving from outside the Internet onto the Internet. That included a great deal of information from commerce, news, people connecting and the like. But what we are interested in here is mostly human knowledge itself. Almost everything known by humans moved from their heads, libraries, archives, universities, laboratories, historical societies, etc., etc. on to the Internet. The big problem I dealt with was what to call all that knowledge—what to call what used to be labeled "academic knowledge," "the 3Rs" and the like back when a powerful education sector pretty much had control of the stuff.

NOTE: At this point in the presentation the first question appeared in the banner across the bottom of everyone's screens. The question was: *Why not just call it knowledge?* To the surprise of just about everyone, Dr. OO suddenly broke

---

4   http://www.iw3p.com/DailyPundit/2001_12_30_dailypundit_archive.php#8315120

off what he had been saying. As he looked directly into the camera lens pointed toward him, he leaned forward.

Dr. OO: My goodness, thank you! A very good question! Old Druid here is flattered to have such an excellent question. And I am happy to answer it.

NOTE: Later private comments were about equally divided as to being most surprised by
Dr. OO calling himself Druid and by his answering the question at all.

Dr. OO: Knowledge, like content, is just an awful word. Content means two completely different things. Knowledge means so many things that it hardly means anything at all. On top of that, there is that large branch of philosophy, epistemology as you know, that seeks to figure out what if anything knowledge is. Frankly, I just got sick and tired of talking about "knowledge content" and then spending a bunch of energy trying to explain what it was.

So I suggested something very simple. If you want to talk about the chemistry that you can learn about it on the Internet, you say it is what you will find online in the chemistryosphere. Historians can put what they know into the historyosphere, Egyptologists the Egyptosphere, people who study spiders the arachnidosphere and folks whose field is the grand old bard go online to work in the Shakespearosphere.

Now sometimes the names sound a little silly, like Shakespearosphere, though I must admit I enjoy pronouncing that one out loud. But much more importantly, people know what Shakespearosphere means far more quickly than if you say something like the online content of knowledge about Shakespeare. When they say something like that there is not even a wisp of a suggestion that all the quality websites about Shakespeare are connected to each other in marvelous cognitive ways. The Shakespearosphere is one of the most interrelated subjects online: plays, sonnets, biography, interpretations, theaters, history—all woven into the one network. The ophere's the thing!

But I am getting a bit carried away. Just know that there is bountiful stuff about Shakespeare out there on the Internet: websites, archives, bases of data, and commentary from experts. Just like the blogosphere, the Shakespearosphere is interconnected, dynamic, rich in resources and a place where new knowledge about William Shakespeare comes and grows and links out to related online materials.

NOTE: A new question appeared in the banner beneath the screens: *Is everything that is online about Shakespeare only in the Shakespearosphere?* As Dr. OO suddenly paused, bets went down in the backchannel pools 13 to 2 that the old Druid would ignore the question. He stared for a while into the camera lens, and then spoke.

Dr. OO: I am going to tell you the answer, but a lot of you are not going to believe me. The concept is very tough to understand. What actually happens is this: when something of value about William Shakespeare is placed online in any osphere, that stuff will soon appear in every other quality osphere about Shakespeare, but it will only actually exist once on the Internet. Nonetheless, it will be available simultaneously in just about everywhere it is relevant.

NOTE: The words *you're kidding* appeared at the end of the question text on the banner. In less than five seconds the text was deleted from the banner. Only Dr. OO had the button to do that. When he spoke again he was clearly miffed.

Dr. OO: I don't mind being queried or challenged. But sarcasm is not to be tolerated. Anyone who thinks I am kidding about the redundancy of the knowledge content of the Internet is naïve, to put it politely.

Let me give you an example. In the old days before the Internet, if an archaeologist dug up a new tablet and translated it to get a new piece of ancient writing, the tablet would go in a single museum somewhere. It might be years before the translation and a picture of the tablet were published. Even after that happened, it would take many more years for everyone interested the tablet become familiar with the new writing—most probably by reading an article or book.

But ospheres have change all of that. Once a new piece of translation is place on a website, it can almost instantly appear in any other website, as a link or as an exhibit in a window on the distant website. Usually, newsreaders alert a global community of interested scholars when something new shows up online. It is quite literally true that when one a bit of knowledge (drat that word!) makes it into the cloud, it suddenly shows up everywhere at once. An early and macabre example of that occurred in the hanging of Iraqi dictator Saddam Hussein in 2006. Someone captured the actual hanging on a mobile video camera and sent the video around to some digital addresses. Within very few hours the video could be seen on thousands of webpages.

One aspect of osphere science studies is the long term effects of the fast

53

distribution of a piece of information. A basic ospheritic rule is that meaningful stuff finds its way into relevant ospheres—and stays there until something more recent and accurate takes its place.

NOTE: Once again a question appeared in the banner at the bottom of the screens: *Is a social network an osphere?* Dr. OO stopped briefly and then began to sputter.

Dr. OO: Oh my, no, no, no! Twenty-five years of explaining and it's always the same damn question! Listen, listen, listen!!! Social networking is among people—great for sure. Ospheres are networks of ideas—of knowledge, of content. In the mathosphere, algebra forms a pattern with calculus and with geometry, and there are links among all three, with geometry linking out to trigonometry. Those links are based on what the content of the stuff that is online means, not on what people are learning about the ideas and what people are teaching them or ideas they are adding.

I realize people think this old Druid is cranky and stubborn. If you want to know why I am that way it is because so many people just can't seem to see that knowledge content is real stuff that forms network patterns just like people do. When I came up with the osphere lexicon the main reason was because those first years of the 21st century people were so bloody relativistic. They were deep down sure that because somebody thought something was true, it was true! They got the darn fool idea that social networking was the way knowledge should be learned. They taught each other to respect what each person thinks, no matter how silly what that person is thinking might be.

Let me tell you just how knowledge really should be learned: learning is done by looking at the relationships within the knowledge itself. How are 2+2 related to 4? Somebody may think the relationship is 5 and somebody else that it is 3. But no matter what anybody thinks, the relationship is 4. No relativism there! The mathosphere online is the collection of what is known about math along with links among the ideas that show how bigger ideas emerge from the smaller ones when they are correctly related. An osphere obeys the network laws just like a social network does. But an osphere makes links based only on what the content means (like 2+2=4). The result is not a social network. An osphere is an idea network—something like an idea in your head except an osphere is out there online for all to learn from. Really interesting stuff.

Same thing as the mathosphere is true with studying history. The historyosphere is the network of what is known about events in history. It is not a network of people who think they know the subject—not a social network. In the ancient Greece area of the historyosphere, for example, there is material setting out everything known about the Battle of Marathon that took place in September 490 BC. The dynamics of this osphere are not about the people thinking about them. The dynamics are the relationships among the facts themselves. What event caused what other event? The way people play a role in these dynamics is by visiting the materials they judge best an ignoring pages about a subject they think are less accurate historically. In that way, the best material gets stronger, has more links to it, and tends to dominate within the osphere.

Social networking is an important part of learning, but so are the ospheres.

NOTE: For the first time, Dr. OO stepped from behind his lectern. His eyes glistened as he rose to his full stature and looked again directly into the camera.

Dr. OO: The getting together socially online to do all sorts of things cannot be dismissed. It is a major aspect of our times. But the individual student, scholar, thinker—indeed individual citizen of earth—needs just as much the rich resources that are the treasured products of human thought and deed. The ospheres are our time's repositories of these grand treasures. It takes no human company or discussion to imbibe individually words such as these spoken by Pericles and given to us by Thucydides:

> Our form of government does not enter into rivalry with the institutions of others. Our government does not copy our neighbors', but is an example to them. It is true that we are called a democracy, for the administration is in the hands of the many and not of the few. But while there exists equal justice to all and alike in their private disputes, the claim of excellence is also recognized; and when a citizen is in any way distinguished, he is preferred to the public service, not as a matter of privilege, but as the reward of merit. Neither is poverty an obstacle, but a man may benefit his country whatever the obscurity of his condition.[5]

These are not words to be changed by social discussion. These are word to be learned and understood by the individual human mind. They are from the sum total of what is known by humankind which is now best stored and ac-

---

5   Thucydides: Pericles' Funeral Oration. http://www.wsu.edu/~dee/GREECE/PERI-CLES.HTM

cessed from the ospheres that reside in our global online commons.

CONCLUDING NOTES: At this point Dr. OO returned to and completed his prepared presentation. He did not respond to any of the several further questions that appeared in the banner. For the over one an a half hours that he spoke, he frequently used illustrations and examples from actual ospheres— personal favorites of his that he had collected online over the past year.

One of the illustrations he described in detail was the small spiceosphere. His main point about that one was how a single very small topic could show up in several different subject ospheres adding important different meaning to each of the different subjects. About the spicosphere, he said:

Dr. OO: You may be aware of the work that has been done in Africa on Aframomum, which has been has been appreciated as a paradise spice for many centuries. A Rwandan scientist named Shema has been working for the past several years on the medicinal aspects of Aframomum. His work has affected not only cardiac medicine, but the vigor of gorillas and their new optimism for their long-range survival, plus, would you believe, Mexican cooking?

So which osphere has the knowledge material about Aframomum? The marvel of ospherology is that Aframomum shows up in the ospheres for ancient spices, Rwanda, cardiac medicine, the new 900-pound gorillas and Mexican cooking. If you go online into any of the Aframomum clusters in any of those ospheres, you will not only learn all about the spice in the context of the subject of the osphere you are in. There will be links there that will lead you to each of the other subjects.

A history student who goes to the ancient spices subject to learn about caravans that crossed the Sahara Desert will find out that on the backs of those camels was a spice that made gorillas healthy, increasing their weight in the 21st century to 900 pounds, and added a zest to Mexican food that was making chefs famous in New Mexico.

That folks, is the wonderful core of 21st century learning. The ospheres arrange knowledge by linking it to other ideas by its meaning. Of course what I have been talking shows still another kind of osphere: the Aframomumosphere, and it is a beautiful cluster of the spice's knowledge that links out to the diverse topics from gorillas to Mexican food. There is no way to draw a picture of these marvels of ospherology because they are more than three dimensional, more than multidimensional. They are omnidimensional and paper is flat.

But with a little quiet reflection, you can see them in your mind. Imagine a spiceosphere that is a network with nodes that have information about different spices. Then imagine in that network a cluster of nodes about Aframomum. Next shift to thinking about the Aframomumosphere that is out there within the Internet. The Aframomumosphere is a network of nodes only about this particular paradise spice. If you imagine in your mind that osphere, you realize this second network has more nodes than the one just about spices and the pattern links to completely different patterns, this time with 900-pound gorillas grinning at you and eager eaters munching tamales.

Once again let me say that these are not social networks. They are a phenomenon of the Internet that is enormously important to the effectiveness of social networks. They give people the online knowledge substance to discuss and connect. But the connections within an osphere are—by my definition and my insistence as founder of the science—connections among the ideas of the subject itself. In and osphere it is the ideas themselves that intertwingle.

CONCLUDING NOTES (continued):
Later when he was home for the evening with his wife, she asked him how his big day had gone. "Druid dear, did they understand?"

He replied, "It is so much more of a popular thing to be a social network butterfly. Content is definitely not king, but I remain its advocate."

Content of the Cloud

Since around the year 2000, the freshest most comprehensive and authoritative source for almost any subject taught in schools and universities has been online. What Dr. OO calls ospheres are real, and have been forming since the earliest days of the Internet. Very seldom, though, do they get much attention. Few people even know they are there. They do not even have a name, so I made up the name osphere.

It is true that most people know and say that if you want to find out about something the best place to go now is by and large the Internet. Finding something on the Internet usually means going to Google or another search engine, entering a few words and then clicking into one of the results the search engine lists. Seldom does the searcher think about the fact that clicking into one of the links the search engine lists is actually jumping into a node on a small network of related subjects. The first webpage you come to will nearly always be linked to other webpages related to the subject, and most of these webpages will be linked to more, and these back and forth among themselves and out to other related webpages. Dr. OO will, according to our look above into the future, call these networked batches of content about an academic subject ospheres.

It is odd—some say criminal—that the education industry has not embraced the cognitive interlinking among webpages. The education industry has largely tended instead to pick and choose some of the webpages for lesson plans, standards and curricula instead of using the clusters of interrelated online knowledge. It has, in fact, been the usual habit of educators to teach students to not trust what websites say without verifying them outside of their own ospheres. Why? The clusters about subjects online are linked together by experts and rise to the top of search engines by their multiple use. As we will see in the chapter *The Cloud is Smart*, distrusting the ospheres is ignoring the cloud wisdom.

As the mobile phone phenomenon has seized the kids, almost no attention has been given yet to the possibility of the mobile devices connecting students to the places online where they can learn. Instead, the assumption has been that the social uses the kids are relishing are by what the mobile device must be judged.

As soon 2010, it is probable that small mobile devices will browse the Internet at least as effectively as stationary computers do now. The push for mobile broadband is vigorous and gaining speed. Devices that project images from the small mobiles on to walls and screens are already in development and new kinds of keyboard input are being tested. The mobile experience in using the Internet may be better than working with desktop machines by the end of the present decade. Beyond is first 21st century decade, the personal mobile seems certain to mature into the worldwide Internet basic connective device. Almost everyone on earth will own one.

The freshest most comprehensive and authoritative source for almost any subject taught in schools and universities is online where it is clustered cognitively waiting for students to explore it.

As it becomes more and more true and more and more obvious that the new generation has a mobile device ideal for exploring these subjects in their pockets, the mobile will take its proper place as the key tool of the individual student for engaging knowledge content.

And for those who prefer to think of learning as a social networking process, the mobile is ideal for doing things that way too—as we will look at in pages ahead.

Network Laws

Geeti and Orchir met in a chemistry wiki when they were fourteen. She was growing up in Nanjangud, in the district of Mysore, India. Orchir had spent his early childhood moving with his nomadic family around the Mongolian steppe. When he was thirteen, he had convinced his parents to let him live with an uncle in Ulaanbaatar.

Orchir had hoped to live one day in the Mongolian capital since the time he watched his father use a white phone, as they were called, in a street in the city. He had come into the city on a supply trip with his father. They had stopped on the street where his father paid a vendor to use the phone for ten minutes to call his brother who had been sent to Moscow to train as a transmitter technician.

The year was 2006 and then six-year-old Orchir's mind was flooded with fascination for faraway places as he watched his father talk. When his father handed him the phone and he heard his uncle's happy voice tell him about the great and distant city where he stood, Orchir's worldview grew from the visible sweeps of Mongolia's steppes, spiced with a few childish urban scenes in Ulaanbaatar, to the awareness that there was a whole continent out there. By the time he was thirty, that first thrill of hearing a voice a continent away was still as vivid as the day it occurred.

The allure sparked by his first distant connection deepen as Orchir grew older and learned more of the possibilities of the time into which he had been born. Orchir learned that Mongolia's natural resources had not been developed. He was intrigued when he found out that in other parts of the world Mongolia had long been synonymous with the ends of the Earth. Mostly, though, he thought about being part of the virtual world he first experienced through the white phone when he was a small boy.

When Orchir was eight-years-old his family got their first mobile phone. It was provided through a program called the Migrate Mobile Market ("MMM"). It was a joint project by SkyTel and the Mongolian government which was put in place to allow nomadic families to interact at a distance with each other and beyond, and to receive weather, market and agricultural information. The mobiles supplied to the families were equipped with the usual 2008 features, as well as some tutorials that family members could use to learn basic reading, writing, arithmetic and digital connectivity. The mobiles had solar batteries and unlim-

59

ited usage. Orchir quickly became the family mobile expert. His father relied on him to keep the data useful for caring for their flocks current, and otherwise let Orchir treat the mobile as his own.

In 2010, the MMM mobile devices families had been using were replaced with new models that included full Internet browsing. The upgraded MMM device connected through a new satellite transmission of the Internet that provided the entire country of Mongolia with broadband reception. Orchir thought to himself when he heard about the coverage, "the Internet has now reached the ends of the Earth."

Soon after the first MMM mobiles were distributed, a network sprang up among the circular felt-covered gers that move in the seasons across Mongolia. Often, as happened with Orchir, it was one of the kids in other families who stepped up to be in charge of the mobile that connected life in their ger to the other nomads and to the world beyond. There were exceptions. The transmitting voice of one of the gers was a grandfather—a man who had been a teacher in Ulaanbaatar for many years. His wife had died and he returned to his youngest son's family to spend his later years in the nomadic life he had known when he was young.

Grandfather, as the mostly teenage mobile handlers for the other gers called him at first, came to be their tutor for the studies they increasingly undertook by accessing learning materials with their mobiles. After his role as tutor had been going on for a few months, his name was changed. He had recommended to one of the eager young women who jumped into a six-person networked discussion of history that she read some Plato. The woman accessed portions of the ancient philosopher's writing, reading it on the newly enlarged screen of her family's 2010 mobile. The next time she was in on a conference with the grandfather she said, "you are wonderful because after we study ideas by ourselves, you can ask us questions. You are Socrates!" The name stuck, and the old man secretly was enormously pleased.

Orchir had realized when he first took command of the family mobile that he would have to keep himself from becoming irreplaceable as the only operator if he was going to be able to move to the city. He carefully tutored his next youngest brother and sister in using the mobile. By the time he was twelve, he realized there was nothing to worry about. Everyone in the ger of every age had a personal mobile and they were all using them like a herd of ger geeks. Even his grandmother happily chatted on and on with her sister who lived far into the Mongolian interior.

At thirteen, Orchir moved to Ulaanbaatar into the home of his mother's brother and his family. His awareness of Mongolia's natural resources had led him into studying chemistry online. At thirteen he had mastered basic chemistry and was eager to move on. His aunt and uncle, who felt a strong responsibility for the nephew under their care, were alarmed when he was offered a paid internship with a gold exploration start-up company. As things were to turn out, Orchir's strenuous insistence that he be allowed to take the position led to his becoming Mongolia's first billionaire by the age of twenty-seven.

Gold was Orchir's first great adventure. The second grand adventure—the one he and Geeti are undertaking at age thirty—began long after their first contact as teenagers through the chemistry wiki.

Geeti is privileged and gifted, and has always been determined to take advantage of all that she had. Her wealthy parents continuously provided Geeti with whatever she wanted, along with a lot of things she discovered to be wonderful even though she would never have thought of asking for them. Geeti's genes made her stunningly beautiful, from her thick, shiny hair to her cute toes with naturally pinkish nails. Geeti's genes also endowed her with intelligence that measured off the top of the IQ charts. Even with all of that—and even in spite of it all— most people thought Geeti's greatest gift was her delightful, warm and caring personality.

Like Orchir, before she was a teenager, Geeti decided to become a chemist. As they constantly did, her parents reacted to her decision with enthusiasm and generosity. Soon she was taken on private tours of India's major chemical installations. A room in the family's large villa was equipped as a chemistry laboratory and a private tutor was hired to teach Geeti the chemical ropes.

Geeti and Orchir first encountered each other in a wiki section on the topic of making gold synthetically. Each intrigued by the other's contribution to the subject in the wiki essays, they soon contacted each other through back channels. They exchanged email addresses and sent messages back and forth. Before long they began having conversations through their mobiles, seeing each other through live transmission on their mobile screens.

In the decade that followed their first meeting in the wiki, as did Orchir, Geeti accomplished a great deal. She acquired some fame by being named *Ms. Mysore* and then *Ms. India*. She enjoyed the attention, and knew she was meeting people and gaining recognition that might be helpful to her chief goal.

Geeti realized in her early years that she was very fortunate. She also knew that she had an exceptional intelligence. It was not lost on her that she could be counted on to score the highest of anyone taking a test. She did not make it known that she barely studied at all to make high scores. She knew people liked her, and she hoped fervently that they realized how very much she liked them.

Geeti's chief goal was pay back. She was determined to give something in return for all that she had been given. There was some ego in her goal. "I have to do something really, really big for the world," was her thought of thoughts in her heart of hearts.

The interest Geeti had in chemistry originally had nothing to do with her chief goal. Chemistry was an outlet for her intellectual curiosity. In chemistry she looked for the answer to how things happened. How could the chemical elements emerge from simpler substances? What caused the patterns of links that formed molecules? Whenever the press of public activities exhausted Geeti, she would flee to her laboratory and tinker with compounds or become lost in reading the entries in the journals of advanced chemistry.

As Geeti moved through her teens and twenties, she became a leading personality in India's emergent 21st century transformation. Her family's wealth supported her as she focused on connecting everyone in India into the online knowledge commons as schools were transformed into nurturing, culture and arts centers for the new generations and intellectual nourishment came increasing from the virtual world.

Three weeks after here thirtieth birthday, Geeti received an email from her old friend, the recent billionaire Orchir. The message said: "Geeti, let's do something really big! Can you come up to Ulaanbaatar and let me show you what I have in mind?"

As we join Orchir and Geeti in August of 2030, Orchir is showing her a panel with an interactive diagram. There are only two types of pieces illustrated: lines and dots. Orchir says, "Geeti, it is so simple. It makes Newton's Laws look complex! Emergence just needs nodes and links. It first happened to me when we got a mobile in every ger when I was eight-years-old. Each of us that had a mobile was a node, and we started linking to each other—and it changed our world. The way we linked made patterns. Those patterns were completely new patterns. They had never happened before. Once they happened Mongolia was changed. When our new patterns connected to patterns from other places Mongolia was not the ends of the Earth anymore."

Greeti looked at him quizzically. "I get that," she said.

"Geeti, why can't we do the same thing to make new pharmaceuticals? We can emerge them, like gold emerged as an element. Instead of testing every accidental chemical mix on the planet to try to find something that works, let's emerge the cures by using network laws. We would be a great team. I may be rich, but I am a ger geek from Mongolia. You know how to deal with people."

Thus a connectivity project begins. We do not know in 2007 how Orchir's idea would turn out. But we do know what he means by network laws. Network laws tell us how things behave in a network just as Newton's Laws tell us how an apple behaves when it falls off of a tree.

Network Laws

The notion of laws being out there in reality is quite a mysterious thing. When we are children, we are told about laws we must obey. Some are moral: do not lie, cheat, steal or kill. What those laws are is proclaimed by religion and speculated about in philosophy.

Physical laws tend to explain themselves. One of them becomes obvious if you fall off a high cliff onto some sharp rocks: you are breaking laws your body demands that you obey to keep you from being broken. Rudyard Kipling summed up this kind of lesson in his poem *The Gods of the Copybook Headings:* "That Water would certainly wet us, as Fire would certainly burn."

As the centuries and millennia of human thought have rolled along, new physical laws have been discovered. A major example is those we call Newton's Laws. One of them explains a lot about what happens if you fall off of a cliff.

Two years before the end of the 20th century some new laws about networks were discovered. Just as one of Newton's Laws says that gravity makes apples fall down when they leave a tree, network laws tell us things like these: nodes link up into clusters with long tails in patterns where any one node can be connected to any other node, and the nodes are located in respect to each other with only about six degrees of separation.

From where on earth or in the cosmos could such laws come? Why everything out there works the way it does is not what this book is about. It is not about why water wets, fire burns or apples fall. It is, however, about a brand new discovery of how things work—one that is giving completely new explanations for a lot that is happening in our world. These new explanations are something the new generation is learning about simply by living in their connecting world. Getting some idea about network laws helps the rest of us understand the mobile tomorrow in which our kids will live as adults.

Scientists tiptoe around speculating that there are laws out there. They always make it very clear that their rules of investigation are actually human theories. Laws, they advise us, are models in our minds by which we try to understand reality. A model is used pretty much like a law until something happens and that model fails to reflect something really out there. Nicolaus Copernicus showed that the model of the Earth being the center of everything did not fit reality, and the science world—after quite a ruckus—move the sun into the center.

A well known law that has so far worked well in explaining how things are is the one about gravity. The classic way to illustrate Newton's discovery of the law of gravity is to sketch a fellow sitting under an apple tree. He has a eureka expression on his face as an apple bounces off of his head. Usually there is a dotted line going straight down from the branch above where the apple broke loose down to the head where the apple struck the great genius. John Conduitt, the husband of Newton's niece, wrote:

> In the year 1666 [Newton] retired again from Cambridge ... to his mother in Lincolnshire & whilst he was musing in a garden it came into his thought that the power of gravity (which brought an apple from a tree to the ground) was not limited to a certain distance from earth, but that this power must extend much further than was usually thought. Why not as high as the Moon said he to himself & if so, that must influence her motion & perhaps retain her in her orbit, whereupon he fell a calculating what would be the effect of that supposition...[6]

Although for three and a half centuries since Newton mused in his mother's garden, physicists, engineers, and bungee-jumpers have pondered, harnessed, and sported with the law of gravity that Newton famously described, the law has remained simple:

> Every point mass attracts every other point mass by a force directed along the line connecting the two. This force is proportional to the product of the masses and inversely proportional to the square of the distance between them[.][7]

The whys and wherefores of physical laws like the law of gravity are matters of speculation and philosophy. The laws, meanwhile, are useful in dealing with the real world. It has been verified extensively that apples and every other object always do fall downward, not sideways—a very helpful things to know.

Three hundred and thirty-two years after Newton's eureka experience in his

---

6   Wikipedia, "Newton's Apple." accessed September 3, 2006, http://en.wikipedia.org/wiki/Isaac_Newton#Newton.27s_Apple

7   Ibid. "Newton's law of universal gravitation."

mother's garden, Steven Strogatz and Duncan Watts sat at a desk in Strogatz office in the math department at Cornell University in Ithaca, New York. They were connecting dots with links. On that particular day in 1998, these two men discovered a pattern that they decided to call a small-world network. Their pattern revealed a mechanism not understood before that showed how many things happen in the real world.

As surely as apples fell downward, not sideways, in Newton's mother's garden, a small-world network pattern emerged among the gers of Mongolia in our future story when each received a mobile phone and they began talking to each other and to the world beyond their steppe. Like gravity, the laws of networks cause real things to behave as they do. The same network laws that Orchir experienced in the connectivity among the nomads' gers apply in the networked connections of proteins as they form molecules. Those same network laws determine whether a disease will spread in a population—whether it will or will not reach a tipping point and become an epidemic.

The cloud described in an earlier chapter would be chaos except for the networks that can form within it. How the order of networks emerges is quite simple and elegant. Just think of the cloud as being made up of zillions and zillions of points, or dots like Orchir used in the panel he showed to Geeti. In the cloud, everything that happens between hardware, with software, among people and among ideas in the cloud is the result of dots being linked to other dots, sometimes statically and sometimes dynamically. In the network vocabulary the dots are called nodes. A network is made up only of nodes and links among its nodes.

As the linking goes on, patterns occur. The shapes of the patterns are like snowflakes, endlessly different. Unlike snowflakes, the nodes in the patterns can link to nodes in other patterns to make larger patterns. As any of these patterns happen, network laws are obeyed. We will see some of the patterns that the laws form as we will look at what goes on in the cloud in future chapters—where we call those goings on intertwingling.

Much of what happens in networks comes about with the forming of the small-world sort of networks and their characteristic clusters: the 80/20 power law shapes things so they a have a long tail; a single node is always a center; hierarchies are of minor significance and intertwingling is rampant; and there is more power and beauty in the connecting world where the new generation is already at home.

Mastering the mathematics and finer points of network laws is not necessary to understand their importance. However to understand the world in which people who are now kids will live the rest of their lives—and are already beginning to act and think—knowing that network laws apply is key. The virtual world that young people have already immersed themselves in is a networked environment.

Although stationary computers are still often used, the mobile device is a far more empowering connection for the individual person into the cloud. In ways impossible for a computer that is locked down to a desktop, the mobile enables its owner to act as a node in the networks of the cloud.

As the young boy Orchir sat in his family ger using his mobile to interact with other individuals with mobiles in other gers, he was a node in a network— as were each of the others with whom he was in contact. They formed a social network. In one of the chapters on intertwingling the social networking in the cloud is explored. In that networking, the nodes are individual people. Network laws apply. Regardless of how large the social network grows, one of the things those laws cause is for each person to be connected with each other person within about six degrees of separation. This principle was at work as Orchir and Geeti met, though physically they were separated by many hundreds of miles— not to mention the Himalayan Mountain. Network laws are a beautiful thing.

Dr. OO would add here vehemently, that just as people connect to make networks, so knowledge content connects to make ideas. People and knowledge follow network laws when they connect among themselves and when they connect with each other. As we will look at more in future chapters, on the open Internet the network environment lets delightful and productive intertwingling of ideas and people freely occur, and that is a beautiful thing too.

The cloud is an environment where network laws apply. Kids with mobiles today are already out there experiencing new small-worlds. The 80/20 law affects their virtual relationships and selects the information they use online. Each kid experiences being a center of a pattern when connected into the virtual environment. They are intertwingling enthusiastically, and hoping you will soon be too. To understand their future we need to know that intertwingling will certainly connect them, as in the cloud they will certainly learn.

One Web

The Virtual Geography Graphers
October 2033

In the third decade of the 21st century, graphing virtual geography has become a major science and art. The methodical plotters who specialize in the science are very different sorts of thinkers than the more artistically inclined people who create the visualizations on the art side. This contrast makes the close friendship of Geoff Gitney and Xiumei Gao a particularly stimulating one.

Geoff Gitney, was born in Melbourne, Australia in January of 2007. Four months later, Xiumei Gao, was born in Beijing, China. Both city kids, with parents who were early adopters of mobile technology, Geoff and Xiumei had each carried a mobile even before they took their first steps as toddlers.

Their friendship began when they first met at the Geography Graphing Gurus Inc. ("GGG") new employees meeting in 2027. As a warm-up activity in the first session of the meeting, a poll was taken to see which person in the room had been the youngest when he or she began carrying a personal mobile device that interacted with the Internet. A cash prize was to be awarded to the winner. All the people in the room, including the top GGG executives, department managers and trainers received a form on their mobiles, as did the over fifty new, mostly young, GGG staff who had been hired during the past six months. The three fields on the form for the contest were the first date of carry of a mobile, the primary use for which the mobile was carried and the person's name.

When all the forms had been transmitted back to the calculating software an alert flashed on the seminar screen, which appeared at the front of the meeting room and on each person's mobile. In large purple letters the screen flashed: "Tie!"

The seminar leader was standing at the podium. She said cheerfully, "How exciting! We have never had a tie before." She then clicked the "details" tab on her controls.

The screen projected two times in large green letters: "March 2008 – diaper monitor." A few giggles began across the room along with some low level talking. Someone in the audience called out: "Who are they?" Someone else said loudly, "Who won? Who are the diaper duo?" Then general laughter.

The leaders of GGG and the professional trainers huddled at the front corner of the room, as chatter spread across the audience. Eventually, the seminar leader walked to the podium. She moved the microphone toward her mouth and said, "Since the winners felt their first use of mobiles was appropriate to enter into their forms, we assume that they have no objection to the announcement of their identities. You will each receive the cash prize. I will now push the winner identity tab." The names Xiumei Gao and Geoff Gitney appeared in bright red letters on the screens.

By this time, the meeting was thoroughly warmed up. Necks were craning to look for some way to tell who the winners were. Some one said "Stand up!" and Geoff rose from his chair, taking an elaborate bow. His bow was followed by applause. As that clapping died out Geoff and everyone else started looking around again. A Chinese guy rose, put his hands on his hips and said loudly, "It's not me."

Not one to miss an opportunity for a bit of drama, Xiumei got up from her seat, made her way several rows forward in the audience to where Geoff was standing. When she got there she stood directly in front of him and curtsied. They then held hands, raised them in the air and took a joint bow. Some prompting from the audience followed, the two winners compared notes and then Xiumei moved up to the stage and used the podium to explain that she and Geoff had been equipped by their parents with identical diaper monitors. She added that the mobile they carried as infants was some oddball 2008 idea for a monitor that could detect wetness.

During the two more days of GGG new employee training, Geoff and Xiumei sat together at lunch and dinner, using the occasions to swap stories about their very similar childhoods. In the months and years after that, they often consulted jointly on GGG projects, he from the science side and she from the artistic perspective.

The science of virtual geography graphing is the study of the structure of the cloud—that is of the overall make-up of the virtual digital world. In 2007, when Geoff and Xiumei were born, very little detail was understood about the potential size of the cloud and the positioning of everything pouring into cyberspace.

Geoff's father worked on computers that were outside of the open Internet. His company was one of Australia's large accounting firms. Everything the computers handled was confidential. Geoff decided in his early teens that he did not enjoy all the security and privacy procedures that were necessary in the kind of work his father did. Geoff announced one night at the family dinner table that he liked connecting things, the more the better.

68

By the time Geoff went to work for GGG, the non-open computer information fields were highly developed and an important sector of the economies at every level. Methodology had developed for the non-open networks to interact in limited and controlled ways with the vast One Web.

But Goeff's love and specialty was the grand open network global commons that was the One Web—the virtual ecology where network laws and the resulting intertwingularity rule. The One Web is a place where everyone on earth can participate and all are equal. The great net neutrality battle of the first decade of the century had defeated special interests and pushes for special privileges for anyone using the One Web. Geoff saw his life's ambition as strengthening and perfecting the neutrality of the open commons.

Xiumei, like Geoff, grew up always surround by computers and carrying a personal mobile for longer as she could remember. Her parents were both technology writers and the household conversation often was about the subjects they were researching. Even in this environment, Xiumei ignored technology and reached for anything artistic within her grasp. She always responded to music and seemed to dance before she walked. By the time she was ten knowledge of color and deftness with a brush made her the star in the many visual arts classes in which her parents enrolled her.

As Xiumei developed artistically through her teens, she was drawn more and more into creating abstract works. By the 2020s, the potential value of the artistic side of virtual geography graphing was dawning on companies like GGG. They began looking for people who could visualize the online world. When Xiumei entered a worldwide competition GGG sponsored for artistic renderings of the global commons, Xiumei's entry won first place and GGG offered her a job.

As we return to Geoff Gitney and Xiumei Gao in 2033, they are once again attending the semi-annual GGG new employees seminar—this time as the lead speakers. It is Geoff's role to layout the basic conceptual side of virtual geography graphing and Xiumei's to inspire the new creatives among the employees to apply their artistic insights to visualizing the virtual world contained in the cloud. Still known as the Diaper Duo, Geoff and Xiumei are a popular team and their presentation for the seminar was enthusiastically anticipated. They came on to the speakers platform together. Each was scheduled to make some detailed remarks.

Geoff began by telling the story of how he and Xiumei had met at the new employees meeting six years earlier. He then asked if there was anyone in the audience who had carried a mobile at an earlier age than either he or Xiumei.

At first no hands went up, and then a woman tentatively stood up. Geoff said, "Thanks for responding. Please put your mobile in microphone mode and tell us your story."

She said, "Actually I don't qualify myself for the prize, but I wanted to tell about my daughter who started wearing one of the new Mobile Monitor Bodysuits just after she was born. I just want everybody to know about that because it saved her life." She went on to explain how her hospital was one of the first to work with Dr. Bae Kim. She and her husband had volunteered to let their new baby be part of a test of the suits. One night after they had gone to sleep their daughter had stopped breathing and the suit had sent an alarm that woke up the parents and also called an ambulance. The parents applied CPR until the paramedics arrived and revived the child. She concluded by saying, "I know the alarm was sent out into the Internet where the alarms were triggered to come back to us and the ambulance. I am an artist, and I want to learn to create visuals of that wonderful place."

Geoff thanked the woman for her inspiration and then said, "Xiumei will have some ideas to share about those artistic visions. The GGG president came forward and spoke privately to the seminar leader, who then took the microphone from Geoff. She announced, "GGG is going to make the same cash award that it did six years ago to Geoff and Xiumei—this time the full amount will go both to our new GGG family for your story, and to Dr. Bae Kim's foundation." After some applause, Geoff again addressed the meeting.

"My role, on the science side of virtual geography graphing is to give you the one big idea that creates the character and make-up of the virtual geography. There have been and are many words for the place we study: Internet, Web, cloud, cyberspace and virtual world. Each of those words, and others flying around, have different shades of meaning, but they all refer to a single phenomenon that is now about fifty years old. Back in 2007, Merriam-Webster's dictionary describe that world succinctly in its definition of Internet: *an electronic communications network that connects computer networks and organizational computer facilities around the world.* "[8]

For the next few minutes Geoff went on to explain that virtual geography graphers work to locate all of the computers and their interconnections that form the massive networking that engulfs the planet. He then came back to the major point of his talk, saying that there was big concept upon which everything else is based. That concept, he said was that everything is connected into just One Web. Goeff said, "Always keep in mind that there is just One Web

---

8   http://unabridged.merriam-webster.com/cgi-bin/unabridged?va=internet&x=0&y=0

with which you are concerned. The phrase to put with that is 'everything is connected.'"

"Back in the 20th century individual computers were each worlds unto themselves, with their own private universe on their hard drive. Each computer owner had to have a personal copy of every software program. The software came on disks that you stuck into the side of your computer so the hard drive could copy it into its own little universe. It was darn easy to plot and diagram how those little hard drives were organized. Virtual geography graphing was child's play then."

"By the time I was a teenager, before 2020, everybody on the planet was using the Internet like their parents and grandparents had used the little hard drives inside of their desktop computers. The Internet was one big planetary computer; it was a commons everyone used. Of course now, our mobiles are how we communicate with what we do on the Internet. But you guys know that."

"One Web is what lets intertwingularity add so much to global understanding and progress. Hard disks in isolated computers can't intertwingle. That is for sure. They could communicate with each other back and forth a little bit, but there was nothing much new in that?"

Xiumei then discussed "oneness" as a visualization aesthetic for virtual geography. She explained that like a work of art—a painting, drawing, musical composition—a network emerges by connecting things until a bigger idea is created as a whole that is more than the sum of the parts. She demonstrated how patches of colors formed larger meaning in a painting by Picasso and how the pattern of connected notes in a theme in a Beethoven symphony emerge to emote different feelings in musical movements. Several of the new creative employees began to get noticeably excited about Xiumei's ideas, but the scientists began to look sleepy.

One Web

What the world will really be like in 2033 for people who are kids today will be dependent in very major ways on whether or not One Web continues to describe the Internet. The definition given by the World Wide Web Consortium ("W3C") for the term is: "One Web means making, as far as is reasonable, the same information and services available to users irrespective of the device they are using.[9]

---

9   World Wide Web Consortium. February 2, 2007, http://www.w3.org/TR/mobile-

This definition can be made a narrow one by applying it only to devices, so that the One Web rule requires that a user gets the same content experience from a desktop computer, a kiosk and his mobile phone. A much bigger idea also is conveyed. That bigger principle is that all users experience the same One Web of ideas and information. No users are privileged; knowledge is an equal and individual user right.

It is not necessary to understand the staggering complexity of what I have called from the future virtual geography graphing to appreciate that the principles of One Web are an embodiment of liberty that is new in the digital age. The notion of One Web was nonexistent when the first democracy was created in ancient Athens. The idea of One Web would have been meaningless to the Minutemen who answered the Alarm after the "Shot that was heard around the world" was squeezed off at Lexington, Massachusetts in 1775. Yet in the 21st century, One Web provides individual liberty that every person on earth can have.

It has become, in recent years, a civil liberty to own a device that connects you to the open Internet—to the One Web in which the same rules apply for all. The more people who can do that, and the more we protect and improve the uniform functions and connections in the One Web, the greater will be the personal freedom on our planet. We will all be able to connect to each other and into a commons of human knowledge and culture never before possible even to envision.

It is really quite wonderful how the Internet offers a way to have a global commons. Geography used to make that impossible. A commons originally meant a piece of land that townspeople shared for the grazing of their livestock. Your cows and sheep had to be close enough to the commons to be able to walk to the place for their food. A commons in a town in France could not be used to feed livestock in Africa or Australia—or Belgium for that matter. The distances were too great geographically.

Yet the Internet now makes it possible for intellectual fodder of course content put online by the Massachusetts Institute of Technology to nourish the minds of students from around the world. Anyone with an Internet connection can browse the art in the Hermitage Museum in St. Petersburg, Russia, or in the Louvre in Paris, or the Metropolitan in New York City—or a multitude of smaller collections as small and specialized collections are offering and adding to online browsing of their treasures.

From locations all across the world, universities, laboratories, museums, individual experts, governments, media and others have placed and cultivate online knowledge to be learned by anyone who drops by from anywhere on earth. In the open portions of the Internet that form the One Web, all of this knowledge is networked into the global commons, available to each person who can connect to the Internet.

The future of our youngest generation will be deeply enriched by their access to the commons. Until they take their places as managers of the virtual world, as Geoff and Xiumei are doing in our story above, it is important for the older generations to stand firm for One Web and the liberty it will give the next generations.

What we need to watch out for is that in spite of the built-in momentum the Internet has for openness, there are those who would wall off gardens for their own profit. The early mobile industry has been plagued with this problem. There are also other interests who argue for their own special and faster access within the Internet. The term "net neutrality" is used as the opposite way of doing things—instead of letting special privileges grab special powers, use of the Internet should be equal and neutral for all who connect.

In the chapters ahead we will look at seven intertwingling ways of the new virtual world. These chapters will sketch something of the life people in the young generation can expect in their mobile tomorrow. These new ways are dependent on a net neutrality, One Web Internet environment. The open, intertwingled, smart cloud and creative virtual world will only become reality if we prevent the carving up of the Internet into closed off sectors and roads that move at different speeds.

I frankly think that network laws themselves are so elemental and powerful that a major and sufficient portion of the Internet will say open regardless of pressures to change that. Explaining why that would be true is far more complicated than we need to be here. But we should take our cue from soldiers at Marathon and the Minutemen of America—and be ready and willing to answer quickly any alarm.

Already, kids are engaging the one Web as a single virtual place where the ways of the new virtual world are beginning to be enjoyed: open, commons, center, six degrees, social networking, smart cloud and do it yourself. These are a suite of intertwingularities that can only happen in a place where all users experience the same One Web of ideas and information, no users are privileged and knowledge is an equal and individual user right.

INTERTWINGULARITIES
Ways creativity emerges from digital connectivity (very cool!)

Open

Kyoto, Japan near the Old Imperial Palace
July 2030

Thinking back to our very earliest memories, it can seem as if the specifics we recall for those bits of our own experience long ago may have somehow imprinted us and shaped our future. Maybe it is the other way around: what we recall from early childhood are memories of things that fit the our interests. If the first possibility is the correct one, it would explain the passions that overtook both Nobuo and Chayna.

Nubuo was practically born with a mobile in his hand and by the time he was six-years-old, as an ex-toddler he was a blossoming geek. He could download ringtones, type numbers and symbols with his thumbs and move images in and out of flickr. Nubuo's skills came to him from two situations. His brother, who is five years older was an avid tech kid for whom Nubuo was a handy, ever-eager student. Nubuo was also born in exactly the right year, 2000, to ride the edge of the mobile boom in his native Japan. By the time he was eight, there were more mobiles in Japan than people. It seemed like everyone had a mobile. Nubuo had two.

Family legend had it that a "flying flower" had floated in through the window and perched briefly on her blanket the day Chayna was born. There were no memories she could think of as she became an adult that came before those with flying flowers, as people in her Peruvian homeland like to call butterflies.

Chayna was born and raised in Iquitos, the largest city in the Peruvian jungle. Her father owned five excellent river boats and made a good business out of transporting visitors on scientific expeditions, business projects and assorted adventures into the Amazon wilderness. Born in 2000, by the time Chayna was ten-years-old she was in the top tier echelon of the Little Lepidopterologists League ("LLL") in which children around the world were capturing butterfly images with their mobiles and sending the images to a commons repository.

In Iquitos, Chayna was at the center of the rainforest triumphs and traumas that took place in the first part of the 21st century. Even when she was quite small, she came to understand that the issues were serious and that very interesting people were trying to find solutions. She learned too that there were some people who were doing things that harmed the rainforest—even endangering the beautiful flying flowers.

Her understanding deepened as her father's clients often stayed in the lodg-

77

ings adjacent to her family home and shared meals with her parents and the children. Her imagination absorbed the accounts of returning Amazon sojourners. If any of them mentioned something about butterflies, Chayna would carefully make notes in her mind. As soon as she had a chance after a meal with such a story, she would send a summary of anything new she may have learned about Amazon butterflies to the LLL wiki and cluster.

Through her pre-teen years, Chayna acquired a basic education online. She felt particularly fortunate among her fellow students of the environment, many of whom lived where the subjects they all studied were not close at hand. Students who lived in cities had buildings and streets outside their windows. Chayna was surrounded by the great Amazon rainforest. Outside her bedroom window were bushes and trees that teemed with birds and butterflies. At night the lullaby of the river frogs urged her into sleep.

Her good fortune went even farther as she often had opportunities to round out what she was studying on the Internet by talking with guests at her family's lodge. She looked for chances when they were bored, waiting to travel into the jungle. When that happened, the eager young lepidopterologist helped them fill the time by answering her questions.

On her thirteenth birthday, her father offered to send Chayna to an internship or knowledge center of her choice, anywhere in Peru. She declined, asking instead to be allowed to go with him on trips into the rainforest to conduct projects for biologists in distant laboratories. She told her family that she wanted to be a direct part of creating the future of rainforests, and that she was in a better position to do that from Iquitos than from anywhere else in the world.

Thus Chayna became a hands-on ecologist for whom the Amazon rainforest was her own habitat through thousands of hours during her adolescent years. Her mother often mumbled to her father: "Our daughter is a Tarzan. Where will she ever find a boy Jane who will see her jungle ways as attractive? Will she grow old only with the flying flowers loving her?" But both parents realized their daughter was happy and that she was using her fine mind well.

Who could know that romance would find the rainforest butterfly girl all the way from urban Kyoto? But why not? A century before in Edgar Rice Burroughs' classic story, Jane came all the way from uppity London to fall in love with jungle man Tarzan in Africa.

It might seem in the case of Chayna and Nubuo that opposites attracted. But it was the opposite of that which proved to be the case. They had a profound common interest that united them intellectually. The rest of the romance was doing what comes naturally.

78

The young boy Nubuo followed in his brother's footsteps deep into digital theory and practice. As he learned more he focused on less and less dimension. Nubuo was drawn to the nano world of tiny digital machines. With his parents' support and his brother's tutelage, Nubuo excelled at every stage of study and apprenticeship.

In his teens, he was enrolled in advanced study sections of the universities that had morphed away from curricula of lockstep courses into seminar formats with knowledge specialists who split time between industrial laboratories and discoursing with students. Nubuo also participated in the university arts and articulation opportunities, learning drawing skills, getting fairly good at writing his ideas and relishing the music sessions through which he became the second chair oboist in the university orchestra.

As Nubuo entered his twenties, he qualified as an experimental nanoist specializing in digital representation. In lay terms that means something like: making pictures big enough for the human eye to see of things that are very, very small.

Nubuo had a very, very big idea on a summer day of his twenty-eighth year. It happened as he was sitting on a bench in the gardens of the Old Imperial Palace in his home city of Kyoto. He was looking at a butterfly who had alighted on his knee. The flying flower's wings glittered in the sun as the lovely insect bent his antennae down to smell the fabric of Nubuo's pants. For all of his visitor's visible enchantment, Nubuo mused that he would rather be looking at its molecules. He held up his mobile and framed the butterfly in the camera finder. He pushed the zoom key down until the screen was filled with the club on the end of the antenna with which the creature was carefully probing a small spot of apple juice his host had spilled that morning on his pants. "I wonder what is going on inside that club," Nubuo thought to himself.

Nubuo decided there and then: imaging an individual molecule in that insect's club would get us down to real butterfly basics. Science could then learn how the apple odor he likes is received from my pants. If we could see his molecules as they are doing things we would understand them a lot better than we do from the static specimens when the creatures are dead. Dynamic pictures, that is what we need.

Two years later, Nubuo was sitting on the same bench in the palace gardens. This time Chayna was sitting beside him. They had met earlier in the day at a reception for the group of lepidopterologists with whom she was traveling. Chayna still lived in her home city of Iquitos, where she was now Media Director of the Rainforest Renewal Initiative. Most of her work was reporting to the world the encouraging, unfolding story of the preservation and reinvigoration of the Amazon rainforest.

The experts who made up the traveling group had come to Japan to see the butterflies and meet people involved in their conservation. On the day he met Chayna, Nubuo had been on a panel presented for the lepidopterologists that discussed "Preserving Nature in Digital Images." Nubuo had startled the audience by saying, "Forget the big pictures. You need to see their molecules to understand their relationship to their ecology."

"Okay," Chayna said to Nubuo as they sat on the bench, "I want to see some butterfly molecules." As she said it, two flying flowers floated down onto her skirt.

"They like you!" Nubuo said.

"I just know what colors to wear," Chayna replied laughing.

"My trick is to spill some apple juice on my pants," he responded with slight look of embarrassment.

"That always works," she said, obviously impressed. "So show me their molecules."

Nubuo held his mobile in camera position, pushed a button or two and then clicked the shutter, counted to ten and clicked the shutter again. "There," he said, touching the beam button to send the image to her mobile.

What Chayna saw on her screen was a ten second video of dots linked by lines. As the seconds passed some of the lines changed position, linking to different dots. She played it three times, twice in slow motion. She finally looked up at Nubuo.

"That is a molecule in the butterfly's club as it is sensing the orange color on your skirt," he explained proudly. "It is a creature of the insect's molecular ecology reacting to a creature—you, through the color you are wearing—of its habitat's ecology. Let's try it the other way. Can you get the butterfly to perch on your finger?"

With the consummate skill of a trained lepidopterologist as well as a daughter of the rainforest, Chayna had the beautiful flying flower standing on her finger within moments. Nubuo aimed his mobile lens at the posing insect, captured another video and sent it to Chayna's device.

She looked at the screen and he said, "That is a molecule in the receptor of a neuron ending on your finger responding to the foot of the butterfly. It is sending a signal all the way to your brain setting off lots of neural action that you are aware of as the feeling of the touch of his foot."

"If all of that is going on," she asked, "why do I just see dots and links?"

80

"Isn't the rainforest the same way?" he responded, "It is all a matter of who is doing what to what. In the video of your finger receptor when a tiny wiggle of the insect's foot causes the dot in the center to link to different dots than before it set off changes all the way up to your brain, and those changes become a new conscious feeling of the little guy's foot."

"The butterfly effect!" she laughed. "Of course it is true. Any change at all in an ecology changes everything else—sometimes imperceptibly, sometimes a lot. I remember once when only a few pollinating butterflies were introduced into an Amazon tributary, within a couple of years the whole valley was covered with flowers. The butterflies were new dots for the valley and they linked enough flowers to each other to tip the valley to blossoming all over."

"A molecule is an ecology, so is a cell, so is your body and mine. My imager can turn areas of living ecologies at any scale into abstract charts of dots and links—of the pattern of what is happening. Would you like to see the ecology of your liver?" Nubuo asked Chayna.

"Not on a first date," she shot back, only half laughing.

Within six months the rainforest ecologist and nano ecologist were married. The wedding took place in the rainforest near Iquitos. Chayna's mother beamed in joy at the boy Jane her Tarzan had brought to the Amazon. Nubuo's brother, who was best man, established a Peruvian division of his digital communications company in Iquito assuring his brother and his wife of continuous contact with the urbanized world.

Nubuo and Chayna turned together to life in the rainforest. They began a long range project of comparative ecologies, determined to record and better understand the similarities between the underlying relationships of the largest and smallest worlds.

Open

Like the industrialists who created the great railroads and factories of the 19th and 20th centuries, the early builders of the computer world carved out their areas and projects and set about to create machines and communications. Computers became the big new industry of the 1970s and 1980s.

The industrialists of the previous century who were the most successful bought or squeezed out their competitors and took control of increasingly profitable industry sectors. That same sort of thing began to happen early on with the computer industry. But during the 1990s, as the Internet emerged pretty much all by itself, something weird began to happen. Open began to compete with things controlled from the top. As open projects began to appear a technology intertwingling began.

These definitions from Webopedia.com explain open basics:

Open source: (1) Generically, open source refers to a program in which the source code is available to the general public for use and/or modification from its original design free of charge, i.e., open. Open source code is typically created as a collaborative effort in which programmers improve upon the code and share the changes within the community. Open source sprouted in the technological community as a response to proprietary software owned by corporations....[10]

Open architecture: An architecture whose specifications are public. This includes officially approved standards as well as privately designed architectures whose specifications are made public by the designers. The opposite of open is closed or proprietary. The great advantage of open architectures is that anyone can design add-on products for it. By making an architecture public, however, a manufacturer allows others to duplicate its product. Linux, for example, is considered open architecture because its source code is available to the public for free. In contrast, DOS, Windows, and the Macintosh architecture and operating system have been predominantly closed.[11]

Open source and open architecture in the old industrial days would have meant anybody who felt like it could have gone into Henry Ford's automobile plant and tinkered with how the Model-T car was made. Taking the idea to its logical comparison, it would have really meant that there would be cars made by the combined effort of a lot of people coming by now and then to make suggestions and/or build a little piece or two. That would not have made sense in an automobile plant of the 20th century, but it works just fine on Linux, Firefox, Wikipedia and many other open projects on the Internet.

The open principle is a core requirement for the manifestations of intertwingling that appear throughout this book. It is, I think, a natural attribute of a network. Openness is not just there, it must be there. Openness or the lack of

---

10   Webpedia. Open source, http://www.webopedia.com/TERM/o/open_source.html
11   Webpedia. Open architecture, http://www.webopedia.com/TERM/o/open_architecture.html

it is a core cause of effects we are observing as the Internet continues to grow and mature. Open is an important operative word in the future of the youngest generation.

Just about everybody has an explanation for the Dotbomb that happened when all those people put all that money into the Dotcoms of the 1990s and then the bottom fell out of the prices. My explanation for that is the investors assumed they could make profits by controlling pieces of the new virtual world as had been done with railroads, steel mills, automobile factories and oil fields in the industrial revolution. The ways of the new virtual world turned out to be quite different. The Internet is most efficient, effective—creating value and meaning—when no one controls sectors, when they are open.

An example of this comparison is the limiting still going on of the learning that can be done by students in schools. It is a limitation mobiles can soon remove. Billions of dollars are spent annually writing, printing and distributing textbooks. The business model here is much the same as the 19th century industrialists, who made profits at each stage of production and delivery. The billions continue to be given to the publisher even though a textbook that is open on the Internet costs almost nothing to create and keep up to date. Millions of students could use that textbook at no cost to anyone. The open Internet eliminates the reason to spend the billions for printed textbooks. The open online textbook would make it possible for ideas and learners to intertwingle across great physical and cultural distances—something that has very seldom been allowed to happen so far.

When all students have mobiles of their own that can access open textbooks online, any remaining justification for spending billions to print and distribute textbooks will be gone. The shock that came when this kind of thing happened to other industries in the 1990s was this: there was no online moneymaker to substitute for the profitable brick and mortar business that had been replaced. This effect was felt by travel agencies, human resources businesses, newspapers and many other enterprises.

Whether this new open way is morally good or bad is not the point. The bottom line is that open is inevitable for many kinds of activities when they are positioned online. Closed competitors wither away. The reason this is true is that the new virtual world does not work from the top down. A Henry Ford of the Internet era does not sit at the top of his product design and production, controlling everything beneath him. Instead the ideas of individuals intertwingle and from that emerges the design and construction of the product. Sound crazy? Take a good look at Linux or Wikipedia to see it happening.

In the open network venue, value and meaning are built by connecting—by a sort of intertwingling we are beginning to understand more as time passes. Instead of distributing textbooks from a central point, the open online textbook invites students to connect to it from any point within the Internet. They all literally learn from the same digital page.

In our story above, Nubuo saw correctly that connection is a crucial mechanism of the real world and of life itself. The butterfly's tiny club was filled with molecules that could connect in different ways to respond to different stimuli and to send different kinds of signals. That connecting follows network laws.

Insight into what happens in networks has been gained in life sciences along with realizing in recent years how the same principles began to show up on the Internet. We are understanding that many aspects of life, including ecologies, are networks. Recent studies have found networks operating in molecules, as Nubuo knows well in 2030. By its very definition an ecology is a network because everything is linked to everything else—everything is deeply intertwingled, as Ted Nelson said. This connectedness is allowed by the essential openness of networks. This openness is a way of the world of for the generation that is now kids as Nubuo and Chayna were in the early 2000s.

In our story, Nubuo gave this key to Chayna: "Forget the big pictures. You need to see their molecules to understand their relationship to their ecology."

She laughed and called it the butterfly effect. They were correct.

Things cannot affect other things unless the environment is open. Anything that cannot connect is not part of the ecology. Within the cloud, closed sections do not contribute to nor benefit from what goes on in the big open ecology. What goes on behind garden walls does not affect the grand rainforest. Only in an open venue can intertwingulartiy deliver creativity and life.

Some big pre-Internet enterprises have moved on to the Internet while acting like they remained in the brick and mortar world. Such is the approach taken by the education establishment. The mistake these enterprises, including education, have made is not understanding the open principle. Being a player in the global online world requires being open because that world is a natural ecology: open is how things are or you are not in the ecology.

A rainforest is an ecology: the intertwingling of its contents causes it to be what it is. Without its dynamic interrelationships, it ceases. The molecule in a receptor on your skin is nothing more than a spec of static chemicals without its parts intertwingling dynamically within itself and with its connections that send messages to your brain. Those messages too are a part of the intertwingles that sustain all life.

84

In the virtual online open ecology, like in a rainforest, both static things and dynamic activity are present. The dynamic activity depends on the static things. Birds need trees as places to build their nests. Flowers need rain to grow. Butterflies need nectar to drink, and in doing that they pick up pollen to move to another flower. Even down to the molecules that Nubuo learned to image, and all the way up to the largest trees, there is intertwingling. That action is open or it is not there. Interacting is a key aspect of intertwingularity and perhaps in a rainforest they are synonymous.

Using just one rainforest here belies the fact that our planet has just one physical ecology. A previously unknown bird or butterfly can drift into the Amazon rainforest from the rainforests of other continents. This explanation from Wikipedia of the term butterfly effect gives more clues as to how openness to distant effects is defined:

> The idea that one butterfly could have a far-reaching ripple effect on subsequent events seems first to have appeared in a 1952 short story by Ray Bradbury about time travel . . . although the term "butterfly effect" itself is related to the work of Edward Lorenz, who in a 1963 paper for the New York Academy of Sciences noted that "One meteorologist remarked that if the theory were correct, one flap of a seagull's wings could change the course of weather forever." Later speeches and papers by Lorenz used the more poetic butterfly. According to Lorenz, upon failing to provide a title for a talk he was to present at the 139th meeting of the American Association for the Advancement of Science in 1972, Philip Merilees concocted *Does the flap of a butterfly's wings in Brazil set off a tornado in Texas?* as a title.[12]

The open Internet is an ecology. A webpage is like a molecule, a small piece in which its elements intertwingle and which is connected to other webpages. A big website like Yahoo is comparable to the biggest tree in the rainforest. The way Google finds something for you in the virtual ecology is to check all of the relevant flaps of the wing of every butterfly and tell you which one the most people connected to—then suggesting those most popular ones to you.

In the open online ecology the intertwingling nature of the virtual world is creating the connecting world that will be a major aspect of the future for people now young. More and more, kids are venturing there to intertwingle among themselves and with the emerging global commons.

---

12   http://en.wikipedia.org/wiki/Butterfly_effect

Commons

Commons Cowboys and Joseph's Tomb
February 2030

"Watch this," Nefer said to Brutus, "it's like tossing a crumb to a school of little fish in the reeds by the Nile. They all dart in to take a bite. But if they don't like it when they get close, the first few back off and then the rest just ignore it."

Nefer was showing Brutus sped up patterns for new webpages about the recent discovery of the tomb of Joseph. The burial site had been found near the Nile River in 2028, and in early 2030 it had been opened. Preparations to enter the tomb for the first time were under way as Nefer and Brutus were meeting in Cairo. Brutus, a botanist from Bosnia, had come to Egypt to participate in the preliminary analysis of any grain that might be found in the tomb.

"It is certainly the most important archeological event since the Internet began forty years ago," Nefer continued. "So far I have counted over ten thousand webpages about it and there is no sign of a slow down. The fact that the tomb of a major Biblical character has been opened affects what is known about history and theology incredibly. I don't know what kind of online tsunami we will have if we find Joseph's mummy, but I am sure it will send surges throughout the commons."

"You mean there may be a mummy?" Brutus whispered. "Wouldn't that mean the actual body of Jacob's eleventh son would be there! Think of the DNA. Wow, the ancestry of King David."

"And of Jesus," Nefer added quietly.

Nefer Hilala of Luxor and Brutus Lavrin of Bosnia are commons cowboys. The spin off from search engines of the commons curating profession was one of the major developments for the online world in the 2020s. The commons curators, who like to call themselves commons cowboys, essentially took over as consultants and guides for finding most anything on the Internet. The search engines continued to do the heavy lifting of the good stuff from the junk. The cowboys did the refined herding, culling and some said calving. The cowboys also became vigilantes against predators on the commons that threatened content quality.

Some of the cowboys became highly specialized. An older French woman named Gabriel Gaulle actually specializes in curating the commons references to the matter of how many angels can dance on the head of a pin. She does some related work in the area of Medieval European dances and knows a great deal about the online resources for nanotechnology. She once told Nefer, who trained with her for a summer, that nanoangels watched over all human technologies—that their infinitesimal size makes it possible for them to be present in the nooks and crannies of any machine or chip. Nefer never decided whether Gabielle was joking or was a mystic, but that did not interfere with Nefer's high respect for Gabrielle's expertise concerning the commons. No online reference to an angel dancing on the head of a pin, or anywhere else, ever escaped Gabrielle.

By the 2020s, wonderful as they were, search engines had hit a stone wall. Their spiders could find absolutely anything in the commons. Their algorithms could put webpages into lists, offering people who used the engines the best materials on the subject they were looking for. Around 2015, the search engines had even come up with a rough pattern interface that broke away from the long-standing list of links that search engines had been displaying since the 1990s.

Some said the cowboys were librarians who had jumped into the cyber saddle, making the big switch to being hands to help with tracing how ideas connect instead of people who assigned places for resources to be stored. Dr. Omar O'Malley, whom we met as Dr. OO in the chapter about Content, is often quoted in his take on the commons cowboys: "The cowboys changed us from searchers to finders."

In 2030, most of the work the cowboys do is sharpening the connecting potential and accuracy of websites. Brutus was put on full time staff by the grain growers when he developed an algorithm that—after years of much confusion—prevented connections of webpages referring to grains of sand from ever linking again to food grain online materials.

If nothing else, the usefulness of the cowboys had been proven by their popularity and their financial success. They usually work as independent professionals who are paid by sponsorships. Nefer receives support from several archaeological museums and displays their logos on her website. Brutus is fully occupied on the staff of the International Grain Growers Association. Gabrielle does not display the fact on her website, but proudly tells close friends that she is salaried by France's largest angel food cake bakery. "They think keeping angels in the mainstream is good for business," she explains.

The conversation where Nefer showed Brutus the pattern like a school of fish checking out a crumb in the water was part of her tour for him of her commons curating tools and techniques. The following week the two of them were to be part of the first team of investigators to enter Joseph's tomb. Their job will be to report directly to the global commons what they are finding as they are inside the tomb. In the days to follow that, they are to track the effect on the formation and connecting of online materials of the facts they report.

The follow-up reports on the connections formed are being done under contract to Google Ranch, a curating cowboy division of Google established n 2025. When Nefer had been approached about the job, she said an overall tracking in the first week would not be possible because the online activity would certainly be to large to manage. She suggested that only two archeological items be tracked and that a botanist cowboy be brought in to focus on any grain that was found. Almost everyone expected grain in some form would be discovered since Joseph had saved Egypt and his family from famine by conserving grain.

"Brutus," she said, "we want to watch what the little fish do. I don't mean fish really, of course. I mean people who are going to start looking at the webpages that will report what we find. I know we can show with those patterns which of those pages are the most accurate. We will make cognoscopes every hour for two weeks of my two items plus something about grain that you pick. When we go back and review the cognoscopes, we will know for sure how smart the little fish are."

Cognoscopes are brand new technology in 2030. The name is derived from scoping cognitive patterns within the commons. There is nothing physical—a cognoscope is not a handheld tool—only a software apparatus located in the cloud. The scoping is a new branch of cognography—the imaging of idea patterns in networks.

Brutus replied to Nefer that he supposed the cognoscopes of the grain sectors of the commons would be boring compared to the commons patterning that might occur if Joseph's mummy were found. Nonetheless, Brutus was very excited about being one of only six people who would be the first to enter the tomb after presumably more than three thousand years. He said to himself, "I've got to be sure to look for grain instead of being distracted by a mummy."

When entry day arrived, Nefer and Brutus sat nearby for over an hour as the two senior archeologists worked together at the tomb entrance to remove the last pieces of debris. Another hour of waiting followed as the team photographer captured what the cowboys thought were too many images, all of which went directly on to the Internet. Finally, the signal for them to form up with the entering party was given.

Nefer and then Brutus followed directly behind the two senior archeologists. Slowly the group moved single file down the slanting tomb entry corridor. Nefer focused entirely on finding two items to feature. She found none in the hieroglyphics that covered the corridor walls. Brutus captured three separate pictures of grain gatherers in the hieroglyphics, sending the images to the Internet where they were immediately displayed on the page of his sponsoring grain company and two partnering agricultural museums.

At the bottom of the corridor there was a door to the right into which first one and the then the other senior archeologist disappeared. Next Nefer went through, and then Brutus. The photographer stepped into the room last and began clicking off infrared pictures in the dark. Following him was the lighting man named George, who gently turned up the power on his digital torches illuminating the scene.

Nefer was the first to speak, "Yes, this is how it would have happened" she said, as she stepped closer to the large stone sarcophagus and peered into it, pointing her mobile with its camera rolling into the emptiness where Joseph's embalmed body had almost certainly once lain. She then spoke into the mobile's microphone sending these words from the Bible into the Internet commons:

Genesis 50:26. So Joseph died, being an hundred and ten years old: and they embalmed him, and he was put in a coffin in Egypt.
Exodus 13:19. And Moses took the bones of Joseph with him: for he had strictly sworn with the children of Israel, saying, God will surely visit you; and ye shall carry up my bones away hence with you.
Joshua 24:32. And the bones of Joseph, which the children of Israel brought up out of Egypt, buried they in Schechem . . .

The senior archeologists remarked to each other that they were astounded to see the great number of treasures that had remained securely in the tomb. "No grave robbers here," the first one said, "not when they took the body and not since. Amazing!"

The other archeologist said, "I have a theory. The Egyptians must have been very impressed by how angry God was with them after Moses escaped with his people. When they came back from the chase to the Red Sea they might have thought the safe thing to do was seal up the tomb and forget about it. Not risk bringing more wrath down on their heads."

"Good thought," the other archeologist replied.

Brutus, meanwhile, was taking images and notes of the multiple items he was finding that were filled with or were pictures with grain in them. He even discovered there was grain spilled on the floor. He took pictures of an area on the floor where grain had spilled, to preserve a record of how they had fallen,

90

and scooped up some samples for analysis.

Nefer was trying to settle on the two items she would feature in her cognoscopes. The empty sarcophagus definitely would be one of them. After some hesitation, she decided the second item would be the small stone frog that was sitting on the edge of the open sarcophagus. She wondered if the people whom Moses had sent for Joseph's mummy left it there as a sign of the plagues that had shaken Pharaoh's will. Maybe Moses himself had been there as the Exodus unfolded. Maybe Moses had put the frog there. Did it have his fingerprints? She knew if she featured the frog the cognoscope would go nuts. She could not resist.

Her allotted time in the tomb was almost up. Nefer pointed her mobile camera at the little stone frog and said into the microphone, "Here guarding the edge of the great stone box in which Joseph's body lay while his people prospered in Egypt is a small stone frog. Did those who removed the body leave the frog as a reminder of the first plague brought down by God on Egypt? Did they leave locusts too, that have long since disappeared into dust? I don't know those answers, but this tomb is certain to tell us much more about the Exodus and the Egypt known through the Bible."

Nefer and Brutus returned to her curating studio in Cairo. For the next three weeks they recorded the cognitive patterns that, as Nefer had predicted, swept like tsunamis through the global knowledge commons.

Within two days grain laboratories had identified the species of the granules that Brutus had removed from the tomb. The expert analysis was done in four labs. The reports of each lab immediately were linked to by dozens of websites. Soon links among the websites that had connected to each of the four labs began to thicken. Within three more days, the accuracy of the report of one of the labs had begun to be questioned and links to that lab's website it began to drop off.

Nefer's video and comments about the empty sarcophagus appeared first in her cognoscopes as bright points on major media websites to which links began stringing out like spaghetti. Some of the strings were links to museums and others to university departments. She checked, and within three days every Christian and Jewish theological seminary across the world was linked to her report.

The little frog, as she had suspected, set off crazy patterns of linkages. Whimsically, the herpetologists got into the act with many otherwise serious scientific websites reproducing images of the frog on their pages. Theologians and historians also began studying the frog and producing online commentary.

As the online connecting and commenting frenzy caused by the news of the empty sarcophagus died down, the cowboy work of Nefer and Brutus really began. They were both expected to provide advice on which were the best sources in the commons for information about Joseph's tomb. As they had hoped, the cognographs made their work very simple. They could tell which sources were linked to by experts.

Bruce said to Nefer over dinner the night before he returned to Bosnia, "I suppose we cowboys are better at this than Google was back when they started it all at the turn of the century. The search engines are really good at going through the commons and finding what people want. Sometimes I am not sure the process really needs us."

Nefer smiled. "We are okay, Bruce, as long as the Googles can't tell a stone frog from a lump of marble. Does that make you feel better?"

"Are you sure Google can't?" Bruce asked.

"Yes," she said. "You know as well as I do that the commons is completely ignorant in itself. It is only a way to connect what everyone in the world knows and has known so that the right stuff emerges. It is only human intelligence that is networked."

"That is quite an 'only', Nefer." Bruce replied. "But it is totally true."

Commons

When I visited Egypt with my parents in 1971 my father hired an Egyptian professor of archaeology as our guide for the Great Pyramids. One of the things the professor said to us, with obvious personal excitement, was that there was a hope that one day the tomb of Joseph would be found. That find would tangibly connect the historical accounts in the Bible of the arrival of the people of Israel in Egypt and of their Exodus with modern archeology and historical dating methods.

If the tomb of Joseph had been found in the 1970s, the world would have been informed by radio, television and newspapers. In the months following the initial announcement, historical and scientific reports would have been printed in journals. Books would have followed that, making their way to specialists, interested laypeople libraries and Sunday school classes. If Joseph's tomb were found in 2007, within a few hours information and images from the discovery would be available on millions of mobile phones as well as flooding into the Internet.

The coming of the commons online has changed the way the world knows things. By 2030, when the story of Nefer and Brutus takes place, the commons

92

will be available to essentially everyone on earth. That means each individual can know everything and know it almost as thoroughly as the experts do. Children of the early 21st century will, in their mobile future, each have that knowledge in his or her hand—displayed, explained and referenced in a personal mobile device by which its owner individually controls his or her use of the Internet and its commons.

The commons is completely new. As Nefer told Brutus, the commons is most fundamentally a way to connect what everyone in the world knows so that the right stuff emerges. The commons is not the mass of wires and beams and light that George Gilder describes; those connections form the platform through which move all the zeroes and ones that carry text, images, sounds and their instructions to their destinations within the cloud. The commons is also not the digital stuff—the zeroes and ones—that carry the code of the text, images, sounds and their instructions through the wire, glass and light pipes of the platform.

Think of the commons as a simmering, scintillating ecology of meaning that the open Internet contains. There is complete openness for the meaning: any idea or fact or opinion can connect to any or all other ideas and facts and opinions—or it can turn away as the little fish do in Nefer's metaphor. These bits of meaning intertwingle, limited only by whether or not connecting makes sense. What is beautiful and true forms patterns to emerge from the commons.

The ecology does not exist physically. That would sound spooky, but it is surely no stranger than saying the ideas we have in our brains are not tangible: yet we know they richly interconnect. In fact, the online commons acts very much like the brain in your head in that you can keep adding more and more knowledge up there above your neck. When the knowledge gets up there it does not get stored in disconnected departments. You can think together about the biology of grain and the story of Joseph saving Egypt from famine, and mix into your thinking the excitement of finding grain in Joseph's tomb. Thinking is a kind of intertwingling.

For thousands of years the culture and knowledge of different civilizations, nations and tribes have been separated and often isolated. Beginning around four thousand years ago, civilizations started to expand their knowledge and enrich their cultures in near isolation in China, India, Mesopotamia, Egypt, Africa and the Americas and smaller scattered locations. Even a thousand years ago the ideas from different parts of the world were barely connected.

By 1971, what seemed like profound connectedness took place when people like me and my parents from far away Texas could stand near the Great

Pyramids and be informed by a professor of Egyptology who was in fact an Egyptian. That would have seemed exotic to me when I was studying comparative history in the 1950s at Northwestern University in Illinois. Geography was a potent isolator of people, knowledge and cultures in my youth.

Beginning in the 1990s, the knowledge and culture of the world's people—including what is known of their past back to the dawn of human experience—has migrated on to the Internet. Because the connectivity online is open, the text, images and sounds that support this knowledge and cultural material can all be interconnected. When a professor of Egyptology finds a webpage that relates to what he has presented on his own website, he can choose to link to that other webpage. He is likely to do so only if he respects what the other page has to say. Thus it is the meaning of the webpages, based on the professor's expertise, that causes the link to happen. He has done a bit of Egyptological intertwingling.

The commons is the sum total of the open webpages that contain human knowledge and culture plus the linkage among those pages made by human visitors. The commons is a network of meaning.

The Internet has often been compared to the vision of the Library at Alexandria, which persisted in the declining centuries of the classical western world. In the third century B.C., Ptolemy II of Egypt established the library in the city that Alexander the Great built where the Nile River flows into the Mediterranean Sea. Ptolemy's vision was to collect a copy of every book and scroll that existed and place them all in the great library. Many books and scrolls were collected and Alexandria became an intellectual apex for several centuries.

The knowledge stored in the online commons is everything and very much more than the Library at Alexandria ever was or could be. The Egyptians collected many books and scrolls, but not even all of the writings that existed in their Mediterranean world. Alexandria did not have the comprehensive writings of China, India, Africa—nor most certainly of the Mayans, Incas and other Americans. The online commons has them all and potentially will have the comprehensively.

The commons also fundamentally out does the ancient Alexandrians by not requiring scholars to show up in Egypt to use their collection. Instead, all of the collection is available on the computer of any individual able to browse the Internet.

Yet the greatest intellectual global enrichment caused by the commons is still another feat: intellectual interaction among the knowledge in the commons. In the online, open commons, knowledge freely intertwingles! Patterns form

94

and concepts and ideas emerge.

At the ancient library connecting ideas from within the collections was purely a matter of hands-on and heads-in human labor. We might imagine a Roman math scholar traveling to Alexandria, disembarking on a city dock and taking a room near the library buildings. He would begin his days of study by walking among shelves of scrolls in different rooms and buildings to collect writings by Pythagoras, Euclid, Archimedes and Aristotle. He would handle many scrolls, sticking his head into them to evaluate their usefulness to his studies. As he sat down at a table before him he would have connected the works of the four great thinkers only to the extent that the scrolls he had picked out sat side-by-side in front of him. This was no small accomplishment two thousand years ago.

In the online commons any idea in any of the works you might be studying can be connected to related ideas in any other work—almost literally for any work ever written by any human any time. There are no scrolls to unroll, everything is virtual. Just like Nefer saw a pattern of little fish swimming to a crumb, you can see patterns of related ideas when you work with something you are studying in the commons. At the Library of Alexandria you had to dig through the scrolls to find related ideas. In the commons they swim toward you. Try, for example, a search engine query for "triangle proof" and you will find yourself surrounded by ideas of Pythagoras and Euclid, and about isosceles and equilateral triangles.

The final chapters of this book, about learning, will explore more how the commons is becoming the grand source of knowledge. Other chapters will look at human interaction within the commons that invigorates culture and mitigates separation.

The commons provides equal entry to all into an ecology of individual and intertwingled thought and learning where young people today already feel at home.

Center

Khaled only remembered Osama bin Ladin's voice. Although his older brothers reminded him often that they had all see the world's most hunted man several times during the months he had been lodged off and on in the high mountain village where the boys grew up, Khaled could come up with no memory of what he looked like. What Khaled remembered was the voice that he heard as the men gathered to play audio tapes and the boys were allowed to sit silently in the next room to listen.

"The voice was soft and frightening," Khaled told Kyle, "but some how it attracted me. It was inclusive. It made me feel part of what he was talking about even though I really did not understand the words at all. The way my brothers and the men listened so intently, nodding and looking so determined—it made the man who was making the voice seem very important. He had electricity, which was something very rare in my home village back then," ending his serious words with a chuckle.

"I guess those men did just about anything bin Ladin told them to," Kyle replied.

"Yep," Khaled acknowledged. "And it was only part persuasion. His thugs would have blown up houses in the village if anybody even questioned his directions. All the power in our valley in those years flowed straight from him. Political power I mean. We did not have electricity. We were cut off completely, living like our ancestors did hundreds of years before. Compounding that, because the top man himself hid out in our village, no one was allowed to go in and out of the valley for many, many months."

Khaled and Kyle are chatting after a foreign policy orientation held for newly elected Members of the United States Congress. Kyle was elected that fall from New Mexico. Khaled is the deputy information office of the Afghanistan Embassy. Born in 2000, the two men are now thirty years old.

Khaled did not have any contact with the world beyond his home village in the mountains until he was nine years old. His education up to that point was strictly traditional, including participating in the indoctrination for young boys directed by the Taliban. When Osama bin Ladin and his senior officers were no longer running things, his older brothers returned one day from a trip to Jalalabad, set up wireless and gave Khaled a mobile.

Khaled had discovered very early that he had a gift for languages. He learned three of them before he was seven. His grandmother taught him a tribal language that only a few hundred people knew. All of those were old and living in the valley's villages. She had begun by singing lullabies to Khaled in the old tongue, discovering to her delight that her little grandson could recite the words back to her, and do so perfectly.

He and she got into the habit of using only the nearly lost language when they spoke to each other. Soon they were teasing the rest of the family by sharing secrets out loud that the others could not understand. Even Khaled's father, the grandmother's son, was often mystified by what they were saying. He and the rest of the family and valley residents used the Pashto, which Khaled learned as well.

Khaled's able ear also picked up a simple fluency in Arabic by listening to fighters who lived in the village while training at nearby secret camps. Most of them seemed eager to teach him about what they were doing. He listened to their tales of war, but when he could get them off that subject he would ask them to show him how the Arabic alphabet was set up. His persistence paid off as he got several lessons out of the fighters. He remarked to friends in later years that somehow he absorbed the letters but not the lust for war. "If the world is 80 percent action and 20 percent talk, I'm in the talk minority for sure," he would say.

From the moment his brothers got the antenna working and their new mobile phones connected to information from beyond the mountains, Kahled's life was centered in the mobile. He was captivated by the connectivity.

His oldest brother Abdul was twenty-one when the terrorists were gone and the valley opened. Abhul could recall traveling to cities in Afghanistan before the isolation that Al-Qaeda imposed on the valley. Abdul had attended a non-religious school in Jalalabad for two years when he was in his early teens. There he had learned some basics about digital technologies. It has been Abdul's idea to bring the wireless connection to the valley.

Kahled begged and pestered Abdul incessantly to teach him everything about the new wireless. Abdul was more than happy to have his little brother assist him. Abdul's vision was not centered in the technology. His plan to was open the valley as a commercial and tourist center. He knew reaching past the mountains and past the awful history of the recent years were necessary to open the valley. The wireless connectivity was the first step in his plan.

The presentation Kahled made in 2030 to the newly elected Congress members was the story of his brother Abdul and the transformation of his home valley. As Kahled said in his introduction: "This is a story of the great success of lifting a high altitude population from the depths of wartime isolation and the remoteness of centuries to a world center of ecoculturalism. Our people are prospering, our ecology is safe and our ancient culture is both preserved and shared."

Abdul, his brother explained, set his goal on bringing focus and people to the valley. He led the effort to improve the roads and brought in a construction team to upgrade the tiny Al-Qaeda airstrip into a viable airport for small planes. He established a study center and invited journalistic, environmental and history experts for study camps. For the first two years the fascination of the experts was with the now vacant Al-Qaeda hideouts and training facilities. When that fascination wore off the experts began to look at the eons of human history preserved in the structures, paths and cave fossils. A parallel interest in the valley environment attracted other experts. All of the studies led to publicity and increasing worldwide awareness of the valley.

The next phases of Abdul's valley development were, in this order: eco tourist camps, increasingly luxurious spas, a large hotel nestled against a mountain, enhancement of winter sports facilities and competition for the Winter Olympic Games. Abdul's personal goal was to host the Winter Olympics before 2050.

The new congressman Kyle Croft was growing up in a mountain valley in the southern eastern Colorado mountains in the United States during the same childhood years Kahled experienced in his valley. He and Kahled had been in touch by email for twenty years before they met in person at the foreign policy orientation.

Kyle Croft's father was a wild life scientist. Kyle did his first overnight camping trip when he was three-years-old. By the time he was nine, he knew a lot about the wildlife that lived in the Colorado Rockies. He knew even more about the mobiles his father used to track the individual animals. Although Kyle learned to be enthusiastic about the animals that were the center of his father's life and thinking, his own thoughts gravitated around the networks of digital devices that increasingly assisted science. His father's specialty was the mobile tracking collars and implants that were placed on animals to study their movements and behavior.

When Kyle was seven-years-old he confronted his father on the subject of a personal mobile. He explained that he wanted to have his own mobile. When his father said he would have to wait until he was older, Kyle replied bitterly, "Every raccoon cub you catch gets a mobile of its own. Why do you deny your own son?"

His father laughed, put his hand on the young boy's shoulder and said, "You win. Let's go pick out a raccoon tracker for your pocket."

"I want a human mobile!" the little boy complained.

"I know," his dad said, "was just joking. You can pick it out yourself."

In the months that followed, the wildlife scientist's small boy became a genuine help in the animal tracking work. As the years passed, Kyle expanded his use of the his connection to the virtual world through the device in his pocket. Although the devices Kyle carried became highly sophisticated as the state of mobile development and his own knowledge stayed that the cutting edge, he and his father never stopped calling the mobile Kyle carried a raccoon tracker.

In 2009, Kyle and Kahled met in a section called *High Mountain Valley* on Second Life, in which both did virtual exploring on their mobiles. Although the number of avatars, representing real people, had exceeded ten million by 2009 and the graphics where significantly enhanced, Second Life still fit this description of itself posted on its website in 2007:

> Second Life is a 3-D virtual world entirely built and owned by its residents. Since opening to the public in 2003, it has grown explosively and today is inhabited by a total of 2,808,346 people from around the globe.[13]

The two boys' avatars had been taking separate hikes in the virtual valley when they simultaneously frightened a raccoon that proceeded to attack Kahled's avatar and take a large bite out of his leg. The raccoon then disappeared into the bushes. Kyle's avatar pulled out a first aid kit, patched up the bleeding leg and administered an anti-rabies shot. Kahled's avatar sat quietly through the treatment. When it was finished it said, "What was that thing that bit me?"

"A raccoon, of course, there are a lot of them in the mountains. And they often carry rabies," Kyle's avatar explained.

Kahled's avatar said firmly, "There is nothing like that in the Afghan mountains—such strange eyes, and the teeth are really sharp."

Somewhat put off by having to be interpreted by an avatar Kyle had his virtual self say, "Hey tell me your email and I will send you some raccoon information." Thus the two boys began their correspondence.

Kahled grew up with a mobile in his pocket and the big wide world in his dreams. He learned six more languages through the mobile, so that he was

---

13   SecondLife.com, What Is It? January 21, 2007.http://secondlife.com/whatis/

fairly fluent in ten before he left his teens. Although he continued attending the traditional school in his valley until he was fifteen, he did parallel studies in the global commons. He was often amazed at the difference in what he heard at the school in the valley and what was to be learned in the commons. He noticed over the years that both the school and the commons were refined so that they gradually came closer to saying the same thing.

In his twenties, Kahled rose in prominence in the Afghanistan Foreign Service. He was delighted to be able to travel extensively. He thought to himself that he was very fortunate to be able not only to reach far into the virtual world but to visit the majesty and beauty of the real oceans, deserts, plains and mountains of the physical world.

On the day of the foreign policy orientation Kahled was eager to meet his online friend Kyle. They shook hands before Kahled's talk and meeting again at the reception that followed, they left together to share a drink. When they had ordered, Kyle reached into his briefcase and pulled out a small package. "Here is something I want you to take back to your valley," Kyle said. He placed the package in front of Kahled who untied the string and opened the paper wrapped around its contents. Inside was a small stuffed raccoon. "Just don't let him bite you," Kyle said laughing.

Kahled thanked him and said, "Kyle you know how to connect with people. You are going to win a lot more elections."

Center

When Kahled was a small boy he lived at the center of a valley hideout in a world where he was connected to family and to terrorists. He experienced the voice of Osama bin Laden as compelling—attracting the men to sit around a machine that broadcast his voice and drawing even the village boys into his circle of influence.

Center is a big and complex concept, in philosophy, science, sociology, psychology and information theory. We do not need to go deeply into theory. It is important, though, to know that in the mobile future, your child will experience the virtual online world as being herself or himself the center of what is going on. Where things are intertwingled, there is no boss at the top of a hierarchy, no category to be boxed into and no sequence to fit into. Instead you are the center of patterns forming around you within a network where you have connected. There is great liberty and freedom for creativity because you are the center. As we will see in following chapters, there is also wonderful social networking where, once again, the individual is his or her own center.

As he grew through adolescence Kahled was at the center of the revival of the high mountain valley led by his brother Abdul. The small boy Kyle lived at the center of wildlife studies in a world connected to raccoons and other wildlife and his family.

We each experience our world from a center that is our self. We experience our self as a node in the pattern of static and shifting networks of family, location, work and play. We each experience a unique pattern based on who and where we are.

Kahled's links to his early world were formed as the family little brother; Abdul connected this same world in patterns fitting to the family's oldest brother. The relationships of Kahled and Abdul with their parents, grandparents, the terrorists and the valley were different because of their unique placements as individuals. For Kahled the center of his experience was that of little brother; for Abdul his center was oldest brother.

What Ted Nelson said applies to these relationships: they are not hierarchical, categorical or sequential, they are deeply intertwingled. We experience life as a intertwingularity from which we are a node that feels to us like the center. Everything connects out from us through the things that are our surroundings.

Our thoughts exists around centers too. If you think about someone, more thoughts link out in your mind from that person. When Kahled thought about meeting Kyle in person for the first time, his mind connected to their first meeting and the raccoon that took a bite out of Kahled's avatar. His idea became a pattern of links among himself, Kahled, the raccoon and his friendship that followed over the years.

All of the above is to lead up to being able to point out that when you connect to the new virtual world, you enter it as a center. As the mobiles our children use begin to connect to the Internet, they enter that virtual world as a node in a pattern. The Internet is not a highway with one way to travel. It is a network in which you are always the center of the pattern you perceive and experience. Although there are countless trillions of other nodes out there the only one that controls you is you.

Something else that has countless trillions of little things is a great Sahara Desert of North Africa. By the 2030s when the stories in these chapters take place, the ratio of one grain of sand to the entire Sahara would be a way to think of one mobile user connecting into the vast virtual world or other connectors and countless webpages, images, sounds and junk. How could one grain of sand—you or me—count at all in such a ratio? How much less, could we have such hubris as to consider that either of us is a center?

The key to that answer is that distance and time do not count. Only pattern does. Your grain could link to a node in Timbuktu, and a node in Luxor, and a node in the Sudan which linked in turn to the Timbuktu node and to another node in Morocco. Every node in the vast virtual desert links to other nodes forming patterns of purpose and meaning. Where your child is connected to the Internet he is a node out there, and what that node is linked to at the time defines what you child is doing, experiencing, thinking and learning.

Understanding your own experience and that of your children as being the center of a pattern is a major and positive clue to the future. The open commons online is made up of individuals who are intertwingled—but not forced into hierarchies, categories and sequence. The power to do things rests in the individual and not in up or down control. That is a root of liberty.

With no restriction of distance or time, as a single node—small like a grain of sand—we each have the capacity to link to the most distant other node and to form patterns among nodes to do things and to learn. When you go shopping online, you link to one store and then another, and within online merchants' sites you click from one product to another. Your shopping is dynamic, forming a constantly changing pattern of links around yourself as center.

When the student in your family looks online for knowledge about a subject she is studying, she forms the same sort of dynamic patterns. The material she is studying is presented in a network matrix. When she lands on a webpage with raccoon information that page will be a center node in a pattern for her as she remains there. Linking out from the raccoon page center will be links to pages on species, habitat, diseases and other raccoon subjects.

We hear descriptions of the new way students are learning online as participatory and self-directed. The basis of these engaging new methods is the network of knowledge that forms around a student who enters the open online knowledge commons. The nodes of knowledge connect with each other cognitively in networks of meaning. The student directs herself through the patterns as she grasps their meaning. That is the opposite of methods where knowledge is pushing and being pushed at students.

Thinking about the vast new virtual world as an enormous expanse of physical grains of sand is altogether false because there is and can be no link between grains of sand—not between grains lying near to each other and certainly not between grains a continent apart, from Luxor to Timbuktu. But all it takes on your browser is to click "bookmark" to link a webpage in Luxor or Timbuktu to you computer and thereby to each other.

The experience of the virtual world—huge as it is—is only for you or your child the few other nodes to which you click or link. You are always the center when you connect to the intertwingularity that is the Internet.

Six Degrees

A Cluster Coffee Café, Angelsey Wales
August 2030

Dillon Dunwoody and Owen Davies had gone to the dark side in their orders from the coffee counter. As Dillon dabbled and delayed before taking his first sip Owen dribbled some drops into his spoon and sniffed. In 2030, the physical effects of the dark side of coffee concoctions had been rendered harmless, but the kick seemed just as real when the coffee hit the human system.

At the mid afternoon hour, the café was filled with customers, most of them, like Dillon and Owen who both are thirty, young adults. Located in an ancient shop building in Amlwch, the café is one of nearly forty thousand Cluster Coffee Cafes—known to everyone as CCCs—scattered in eighty-two countries on all seven continents. The CCC in Antarctica is in the Mt. Erebus Resort managed by Aada, whom we met in the chapter about the Cloud.

The CCC business plan has two features to which the success of the coffee chain is attributed. One is the venerable idea of a convivial place to drink coffee—an institution as old as the native American pre-Columbian enjoyment of coffee. Interesting tasting coffee served a hospitable place provides this feature, and CCC is extremely good at doing that. What Dillon and Owen thought of as the dark side was to mix potently some of the exotic coffee strains and add-ons.

The second feature is something of an outgrowth of the wireless hotspot idea that the Starbucks company had offered to its coffee drinkers early in the history of the Internet. Long before 2030, wireless transmission of the Internet had been painted over the entire surface of the earth. Connecting wirelessly to the Internet is open and free in 2030. Almost everyone carries a mobile which is the nearly universal individual tool for dealing with anything that transpires within the One Web of the Internet.

The Cluster Coffee Cafes offer their clientele cluster membership and linking to other CCC clusters. CCC is a small world network that has earned the worldwide nickname: coffeeosphere. The idea that came out of a very long night of coffee drinking in 2025 was that coffee houses filled with drinkers were clusters of people. The group from which the idea emerged that long night were several recent graduates of a business school in Massachusetts. They were bored with the traditional business plans that they had been taught and wanted to come up with something new.

At two o'clock in the morning, one of the graduates blurted out: "If we had coffee houses all over the world, every coffee drinker in every one of them at one time would be separated from every other coffee drinker in every one of them by one degree. How cool it would be if we could let our customers connect with each other while they are drinking coffee, and buying more and more coffee because they are having fun!"

"Of course," another graduate burst in, "since we already have the clusters, why not let the customers entertain themselves by making the connections between clusters. That gives them hundreds of thousands of possible contacts instead of just a couple of dozen in the café cluster where they are sitting. We won't care what they link up about. We will just give them a way to link up!"

All of the graduates who had been in on the overnight coffee binge are now billionaires. Rumor has it that none of them partake in coffee any more, with the possible exception of one decafe drinker.

The networking method the graduate geniuses came up with begins with a large world map that is an interactive screen filling a wall somewhere in each CCC location. The screen is always placed where everyone in the café can see it. On the map a light shines for each CCC in the world. A customer can send a mobile beam at any light and simultaneously sending a few word tags to that location. The tags sent to any CCC location can be displayed by any coffee drinker at that location on his or her mobile. The number of distant people sending a single tag determines how big the text is of that particular tag on a large orb that displays the tags above the map.

The mobile screens of coffee drinkers playing the game also shows links between the CCC locations where the same tag is displayed. Any person in any CCC can send a text message to a tag word displayed for any location. That message then appears in the mobile of each person at the distant location who beamed the tag word to the location.

During the late 2020s extensive analysis has taken place of the results of the Coffee Cluster Café networking. Network theorists have published material describing the links between the clusters as small-world theory weak links. Whether or not the research was meaningful, the cafes became a craze of the decade.

In 2029, a popular psychology magazine documented a wave of inter-country marriages attributed to CCC. The research investigated how tags such as "doglover," "broccoli," and "herpetology" had led to marriages. Of 1,213 marriages documented, only 24 took place between the two coffee drinkers in separate locations who got in contact through a posted tag. The rest were marriages between two individuals connected by the tag contact but about six degrees

106

separated through friends of the coffee drinkers who connected the tages.

A "doglover" tag that was traced was posted in Potsdam by a woman whose brother operated a kennel outside of Paris, France. In a CCC in Fresno, California, a woman who raised poodles responded to the post and began exchanging emails with the Potsdam sister. They conspired a bit about the unmarried brother in Paris, deciding that a poodle dealer that the Fresno woman knew in France should introduce the brother to a canine stylist the French woman hired for her dogs. The brother and the stylist clicked and were married. Counting it up, their were six degrees of separation that were linked as a result of the connection between the Potsdam and Fresno coffee clusters: Unmarried brother-Potsdam sister-"doglover" tag-Fresno dog poodle woman-French poodle lady-canine stylist.

The broccoli tag connected a romance by linking up similar degrees of distance until a Brooklyn bureaucrat and Belgian barber met and fell in love. The herpetology connections slithered through some snake specialists, hopped to an appealing frog expert and led to a wedding in a salamander habitat in Hawaii. Once again, the individuals who eventually met and married were connected by about six degrees through the jungle of online coffee contacts.

As Dillion and Owen continued to put off drinking their coffee and began beaming tags at map targets, a discussion was going on among a cluster of fleas who were chatting in the thick fur on the back of a sheepdog who was sitting under the table. The subject of the fleas' discussion was a Scottie dog sitting under the next table. The Scottie, who belonged to a couple on holiday from Glasgow, was sound asleep and unaware of the conspiring fleas.

"We should send the six sisters," said a large authoritative flea. "They can lay enough eggs to turn that Scottie into a flea farm in a week. By the time the family is back in Scotland that dog will re-establish our race in his neighborhood."

"Yeah, and that would be fair play," said a nearby adult flea. "The poor fellow who popped over here when the Scottie hit town was a sad case." He went on to retell the story of a nearly dead flea who had managed to jump on their dog when the Scottie arrived and came over to smell his rump. The flea told of a powerful powder that had been shaken all over the Scottie before the family left home. The flea survived by hiding in an ear crease, but was terminally ill by the time he made his escape on to the sheepdog. His last hours had been pleasant after his new hosts helped him to a blood meal. But he succumbed in his sleep to the poison remaining in his system from the powder.

The six sisters were thrilled. They were strong, they were pregnant and they were hungry. As the rest of the flea cluster crowded around to give them advice and encouragement, they moved up to the surface of the sheepdog's heavy fur and sat down on a large burr caught in the fur. Once the sisters were in place on the burr, a biting team of nine fleas moved under the fur to the sheepdog's ear and under the ear flap. Counting down from four, the nine fleas simultaneously chomped hard on an unprotected, very sensitive piece of skin near the dog's ear entry.

"Yelp!" screamed the sheepdog as he leapt to his feet. The Scottie woke up with a start and got up. He walked over to his new friend and they sniffed noses. The Scottie then turned to go back under his table as his master called him with a low whistle.

"Now!" the six sisters yelled as they jumped with all their might toward the Scottie. Although they all landed safely on his fur, they were separated at first. By prearranged plan they met on his left side near the soft edge of his belly. After a quick greeting they settled in for their blood drink. They did not bite simultaneously and sunk gently into the flesh. Soon they began to swell in size and purr. (Because they do so very quietly, it is little known that fleas purr when contented.) In the weeks ahead the six sisters looked forward to a pleasant life of more meals and of laying many, many eggs.

Above the table beneath which the sheepdog had now gone back to sleep, Dillon and Owen were facing up to drinking their brews. Dillon took a large swig and suddenly looked ill. Not to be outdone, Owen drank deeply too. Dillon noticed that though Owen managed not to grimace, his eyes crossed slightly.

"I don't know why we all do this. It's crazy," said Dillon, taking and swallowing another large gulp. "We must be trying to prove something—macho, I guess."

"You're right," Owen mused. "There must be a better use for this awful stuff. Maybe it would make good flea poison. Nothing else seems to be working on our big infestation of the little beasties in Wales this season."

Dillon and Owen could not hear the tiny voices beneath their table saying, "Those guys better not do any testing on our sheepdog. We've got transportation to Scotland two jumps away."

Six Degrees of Separation

Fleas are consummate experts at riding the principle of six degrees of separation. The cluster of fleas on the sheepdog linked out through the six sisters who will make a new cluster on their Scottie. The cluster on the Scottie will send a few jumpers to a next dog and a next. The capturing of life that made the business school graduates into billionaires was the implementing of degrees of connectivity among the clusters of coffee drinkers at different café locations. The principles upon which the coffee company and the fleas achieved their prosperity are very real, and very recently understood.

In 1998, Stephen Strogatz and Duncan Watts recognized what they called small-world networks, as we saw in the chapter on Network Laws. These networks are formed by clusters of closely linked nodes with a few links between the clusters. Without this principle the Internet—the entire virtual world out there in cyberspace—would be nothing more than an amorphous stretch of sand like the Great Sahara Desert.

In physical life we are all members of clusters of friends, family, coworkers and other groups with whom we share activities. If you happen to be in a group that raises Scottie dogs, you are connected to each member of the cluster of that group of doglovers by one degree of separation. If one of the members of your cluster is acquainted with a person who breeds Scotties in Glasgow, you are connected to the Glasgow breeder by two degrees: first from you to the friend in your cluster, then from him to the guy in Glasgow. Of course the guy in Glasgow also belongs to several clusters there, so that any person in any of his clusters relates back to you with only three degrees of separation.

An elegant and simple way to conceptualize about how the Internet is set up—how things are linked in the digital cloud that engulfs our planet—is to visualize the Internet as the large world map on the wall of a Coffee Cluster Café. Each light on the map is a cluster. There are lots of nodes in each cluster and each of those nodes can link out to a node in a distant cluster. When that happens, each of the other nodes in both of the clusters where the link has been made are suddenly separated by only two degrees. If Aada in the Antarctica CCC sends a text message to Owen in the Anglesey CCC, anyone drinking coffee where Aada is can ask her to send Owen a request to ask a question of anyone drinking coffee in his cluster.

The mobile tomorrow will not be the chaos of random linking nor the hierarchical, categorical, sequential environment of regular patterning. It will be filled with clusters and links among them. The individual will belong within clusters and connect by degrees through other clusters. Our children are experiencing small-world networks already with their mobiles.

Social Networking

Super Bowl LXIV
February 2030

It surprised no one that the Dallas Cowboys once again won their way through the professional football regular season and the playoffs to be, for the fifteenth time, competing in the Super Bowl. The big surprise was that the Cowboys would be playing the Online Satellites. It seemed incredible that a team less than a decade old and with no city fan or money base to support it could be playing in the championship game.

"Go figure!" That is what the marketing manager for the beer company that is the Super Bowl's major sponsor said when Satellite quarterback Jimbo Jones tossed the winning pass into the hands of his favorite target Wilbert Warner in the last seconds of the playoff.

The frustrated marketing manager's wife put her hand on his knee. "This may be the big one for you, sweetheart," she purred. "Imagine a Super Bowl beer market in every city, town and wide spot on the Interstates—there are Satellite fans everywhere!"

The emergence of support from online for a professional football team had its roots in the fantasy football craze of two decades earlier. In intervening years broadband mobile—and more importantly the projectors in the mobile devices that painted external screens and any handy wall with all the action from the playing field—made following football emitted by personal digital devices increasingly exciting.

In 2024 a franchise was put together drawing support from the virtual world that had be kicking around the idea of having its own a real team supported by online fans. The virtual world, which was part of the Second Life Universe, had for six seasons sported increasingly exciting avatar football leagues that were followed avidly by millions of online fans. By hiring living players, one of those avatar teams was morphed into flesh and blood in an out of the ordinary reversal of the human to avatar replication.

Without a city, the Online Satellites football team's biggest challenge was finding a field to play on. When the franchise opened for investment through the virtual world's bank, within two weeks it raised twice the amount it had targeted. The bountiful cash solved the problem of where to play. The Satellites pays handsomely to use the fields and domes of other teams on weekends when they are out of town.

111

Although Online Satellite supporters living near the stadium where the team is playing each week have increasingly filled the stands, fan support remains primarily remote, piped in from live two-way streaming of the game into the Internet. Audio from fans watching on their mobile, home theater or sports bar computer screens is picked up by microphones and the combined sound is broadcast through stadium loudspeakers during the games.

The first season the players only had the audio support. The second season and thereafter, two story high montages of screens have been set up in stadium seating areas and images are displayed as they are incoming from a spectrum of the fans enjoying the game through the Internet. By the mid 2020s, two-way imaging had become a powerful medium. The incoming remote support for the players had become a factor in the games, and began to be replicated by other teams to supplement the live cheering from fans seated in stadiums.

Although the virtual support of a large national fan base is clearly a factor in winning games, analysts agree that the networking among the players is the secret to the Satellites' success. The players on the Satellite team were born early in the 21st century and have grown up with the networking world. They are nurtured and coached by the highest standards of the social networking methods developed and refined in the first decades of the 21st century.

Satellite coach Larry Linkster played football at a large, diverse urban high school from which he graduated in 2007. Although a boy small in stature and white, Linkster proved invaluable to his high school football team and his school. An expert brought in to analyze the school recognized that little Larry was critical to the reduction of conflict at the complex school. "He moves between black, Asian, Hispanic and white groups, and he's one of these kids who's always bringing good news," the expert said. "He's a very important person in this school."

Larry Linkster loved football but he realized that he was not big enough to become a professional player. He chose a attend a small college where he could be on the football team and where he could major in social networking theory. When he graduated he began at the bottom as a trainer for a professional football team and started working his way up toward his goal of coaching.

Not a lot of coaches were tempted by the new team without a city, but when the Satellites interviewed Linkster his enthusiasm won him the job. Recruiting a team for the first season could have been relatively simple if the newly hired coach had been willing to pay the large salaries the franchise owners had sketched into the budget. But Larry was looking for more than guys who wanted a Ferrari in every town. When the major sponsor marketing manager complained to Larry over beers during the second season that bigger names on the team would sell more beer, the coach narrowed his eyes and said, "Winning the Super Bowl will sell more beer."

To anyone who asked him, Larry would say that his theory of coaching football was to hire men who could do their job well and then to nudge them into networking. "The whole is more than the sum of the parts," he would add.

As the seasons passed and the Satellites began winning more and more games, quarterback Jimbo Jones and Wilbert Warner who caught most of Jimbo's passes emerged in the public perception as the critical stars of the team. Linkster knew better. There were two other players, one an offensive lineman and the other a defensive tackle, who were the catalysts of the team social network. They moved among the players always bringing good news. They energized the network and that caused victories.

Larry understood his two catalysts because he saw himself in them. He knew the satisfaction of being the node in the network of a large high school where he was critical to good results for everybody. He knew that his key guys did not care about the publicity. They enjoyed seeing Jimbo and Wilbert get the headlines because that meant the Satellites were winning.

As the cameras panned the pandemonium on the field following the Satellite Super Bowl LXIV win, the director held the live picture for over a minute on two grinning players sitting together on the winning team bench. They were surrounded by the rest of the team which was taking turns slapping them on their heads and back. Unnoticed by any of the rest of the team Jimbo Jones and Wilbert Warner crept up from behind the bench with a lifted barrel. The camera closed in as they tipped gallons of Gatorade over the two players.

Back in his den, the major sponsor beer marketing manager growled, "We had a barrel of beer ready for them and they picked up the Gatorade again. Hang tradition!"

His wife looked over at him sympathetically, and puzzled. "Why didn't they dump it on their coach?"

The disgruntled manager shot back, "You can be sure that fool coach doesn't care about something like that. He just likes to win."

Social Networking

Better and better understood in recent years, social networking underlies a very great deal of what happens in human affairs. But allowing people to network has not always been appreciated or come easily. We could paraphrase Ted

Nelson: tyrants and management theorists over the centuries keep pretending they can make people hierarchical, categorizable and sequential when they can't. People are naturally intertwingled.

People are pushed into being hierarchical, categorized and sequential when they are enlisted into the military. The chain of command is not questioned. Orders come from the top down and disobedience is not tolerated. They say that on the battlefield top down command and marching in ranks is required to win. Guerrilla fighters from the Minutemen of the American Revolution to the streets of modern Baghdad would point to exceptions to that conclusion.

In the height of the 20th century corporation dominance, every business had a hierarchical organization chart with the Chief Executive Officer in a box at the top, a set of boxes in a horizontal row beneath that for department heads and then more boxes beneath those for managers and descending ranks of lesser employees.

When the Internet began to grow in the mid 1990s, websites had organization charts that looked just like the corporation charts, with the homepage in the CEO box and lesser pages in ranks below that. Perhaps history will look back to say that the obvious meltdown of the hierarchical websites imposed on the digital networked world made us look at the corporate world to see if we were making the same mistake there.

However it occurred, social networking became a hot topic in the early 21st century. Corporations began to realize that what was really happening among all those neatly drawn boxes was usually not going up and down the hierarchy. Real people in real companies communicated in networks through which the power patterns overrode the little boxes. A lot of the times a guy in a lower box was having impact in odd directions and the expected neat flow up and down just was not there. Planning pencils came out and nodes started getting connected to links: social networking was getting put down on paper.

This book is not the place to explore social networking in business or broader theory. But a general understanding that the new virtual world is itself a network is important. The virtual world of our children's tomorrow is a natural network environment in which social networking is platformed effortlessly.

Larry Lingster is based on a real kid in a real high school. We find him in a report that comes from Valdis Krebs,[14] an expert on social networking as it affects, among many things, coaching a winning team in sports. In his blog Net-

---

14   Valdis Krebs, Network Weaving. http://www.networkweaving.com/blog/2006/08/weaving-team-nets.html

work Weaving,[15] Krebs cites this story that appeared in the New York Times in March 2005 about the networking among players on the New York Yankees baseball team:

"So much of psychology and sociology emphasizes the importance of communicating and creating strong bonds to improve group performance, but in a lot of situations that is just not how it works," said Dr. Calvin Morrill, a professor of sociology at the University of California, Irvine, who has studied group behavior in competitive corporate situations and in high schools. "Baseball is an odd mix of an individual and team sport, and an ideal example of where a diffuse team with weak ties to one another may help the overall functionality of the group."[16]

Later in the same article is the inspiration for the two Satellite players on whom the Gatorade was dumped and for Larry Linkster who coaches the Satellites to their Super Bowl LXIV victory:

Whether such independent, loosely tied people ultimately succeed as a unit depends not only on strong management, researchers say, but on the presence of individual group members who can circulate through disparate parts of the team, reduce conflict and help generate collective spirit when it is needed.

In one continuing investigation of a highly diverse high school of 1,600 students, Dr. Morrill found that a single 16-year-old white skateboarder had been critical to the reduction of conflict. "He moves between black, Asian, Hispanic and white groups, and he's one of these kids who's always bringing good news," he said. "He's a very important person in this school."

There is no hierarchy, category or sequence guiding the way the skateboarder moves between the different kids in his school. He is a node in a network who makes patterns of links that create positive feelings and actions. Larry Linkster's two key players did the same thing in the Satellite team that won

15   Network Weaving. http://www.networkweaving.com/blog/

16   New York Times. Close Doesn't Always Count in Winning Games, March 7, 2005. http://www.nytimes.com/2005/03/07/sports/baseball/07psych.html?pagewanted=1&ei= 5088&en=eda8081a39f14d22&ex=1267938000&partner=rssnyt

Super Bowl LXIV. Other nodes in that team network were quarterback Jimbo Jones, Wilber Warner who could catch passes, the rest of the players on the team and of course coach Linkster. The sort of social network within the team that generated the victory is a fundamental human intertwingling that we all know and experience.

Social networking is part of many topics in this book. It is the platform for the cloud wisdom and the do it yourself creativity that are explored in the next two chapters. Social networking is most of what people do when they connect with each other online because the venue they enter is a network.

It is useful to add that social networking is intertwingling, which tells us that we do not just move from one node to the next. We form patterns. Things happen. We connect with other people. Energy is generated. Ideas form. Community grows. Action is discussed and taken. Things are done. Relationships are built. All of those things are part of the intertwingularity inherent in social networks.

When our children use their mobile phones today, they are participating in and building social networks. To understand their mobile tomorrow we need to look at the rich intertwingling that they will enjoy in their social networking and through which they will in significant part build their future.

The Cloud Is Smart

The History of Stone Town
July 2030

Vasco Meghiji was born in 2000 in Stone Town on the island of Zanzibar. Like millions of children his age in all parts of the world, by the time he was a teenager he was interacting with a much broader world than his island home through his mobile device's connection to the Internet cloud.

Vasco was not drawn to the technical side of the emerging digital world as were many of his friends. Vasco became instead more and more deeply fascinated by how the device in his hand could give him information. Where did the information really come from? Was it true? How could he be sure it was false or true? Wondering about that led him into a shadowy time of doubt and then to the project that was to make Stone Town a bright star in the increasingly smart virtual cloud engulfing planet earth..

As Vasco was growing up, Stone Town was a place to get a lot of different versions of what was supposed to be true about the place. When he was thirteen Vasco started checking into the history of his hometown and he was dismayed by the confusion his inquiries caused.

His investigation of Stone Town history began as a project for the AllAfricaWiki history where Vasco hoped to sign on as a junior editor. The new junior editors were required to write and submit a brief history of their hometown in order to qualify to participate in other editorial work. Vasco began his history of Stone Town by scouring the Internet. He found just repetitive entries with the same few facts.

Vasco's suspicions were raised. Why was there not much Stone Town history online? The hotels had some history on their websites, but the stuff they had gave few real facts and just seemed to try to make the hotel welcoming. The tourist websites said very little more. He decided to research the history for himself right there in Stone Town.

Vasco started with his grandfather, who proudly spoke of his Portuguese heritage. His grandfather repeated his usual story about how the family had given Vasco his name in honor of the great Portuguese explorer Vasco de Gama. The boy listened more intently than he had in the past to his grandfather's explanation of Stone Town as essentially a place of important European heritage through the colonial era. "Stone Town was a significant stop on European trade routes with the East," his grandfather said. "That should be the main theme of your report. Vasco de Game himself set foot here."

As he sat alone gazing toward the Indian Ocean and pondering what to do next for his report, Vasco admitted out loud, "No one but Grandfather has ever told me the Portuguese being in Stone Town amounted to a hill of clove buds." He puzzled about what really might be the most important aspect of the history of Stone Town. He decided that if the Europeans were the big factor, the guides at the main tourist center would know. "Those guys mainly show Europeans around," he thought. "I'll ask them."

Vasco rode his bike to the tourist center. When he got there he noticed that two of the chief guides were sitting in the shade outside the office looking bored. The men were friends of his father's. He approached them and asked if they would answer a question for him. They stirred a bit and nodded. Fifteen minutes later, Vasco walked away very confused. The guides had told him that any history from the Portuguese colonial days had been overshadowed by the glamorous era of the sultans. They talked about all the buildings in Stone Town that had been built by the sultans. "If you want something that is important about the Europeans," one of the guides added, "it is the house were Dr. Livingstone stayed before his last trip into Africa."

Over the next few days Vasco visited fourteen other people who had some claim to knowing the history of Stone Town. The more people he talked to the more of a jumble he had in the notes he had been typing on his mobile into his sandbox on the AllAfricaWiki where he felt his chances were dimming of being accepted as a junior editor.

The day after his last interview Vasco dug around in the piles of notes. He began to realize that he could write several different histories of Stone Town depending on which persons he took as authority for what he wrote. He could make Stone Town into a stepping stone from Europe to the Middle and Far East. He could describe Stone Town as a doorway into Africa. He could show Stone Town as the heart of an island ripped away from early human populations and stolen from unique animals who knew it as their only home. He could glamorize Stone Town as an exotic center of the clove trade. He could feature the fabulous architecture and portray the Stone Town of the Sultans.

"How," wondered Vasco, "can I do all of that?"

"More important," he worried, "what is true and what is not?"

After worrying about his dilemma for a week, Vasco sent an email to the chief of the junior editors at the AllAfricaWiki withdrawing his application for a position. The chief who received Vasco's resignation was Melba Muthemba of Mozambique. She sighed sadly, thinking the project may have missed a talented kid. Lingering with the email to read it a second time, she thought, "Odd name. Where did Vasco come from on Zanzibar?"

Two years later Melba Muthemba was taking a holiday in Zanzibar. She walked from her Stone Town hotel to the tourist center to begin the guided walk through the old city's streets. As she stood in the shade outside the office with the three others who had signed up for the tour, a serious young man wearing a guide badge in his hat came out off the building and joined them. He said to the group, "I am your guide this morning. My name is Vasco Meghiji. Please call me Vasco."

Melba did a double take. At first she did not know why the name surprised her. Then she remembered that Vasco was the name of the Zanzibar boy who had withdrawn from the wiki. "Six degrees of separation," she mused. "If this is the boy, it is a lot less than six degrees!"

At the walking tour's first rest stop, as the group sipped fruit juice on a porch of the Old Dispensary, Melba asked Vasco if he had been the applicant who had withdrawn. He admitted that he was, trying to control his embarrassment. Melba was inclined to worry as much as Vasco was, and she became immediately concerned that the wiki had not been fair to Vasco. After a lot of mutual apologizing, the two realized they had a great deal in common. A strong understanding between them was born and the history of Stone Town was suddenly in very competent hands.

Melba Muthemba was old enough to be Vasco's grandmother. She had personally seen a great deal of history and change in Africa. Born in 1954, she could remember the chaos from the end of the colonial era. She had lived through wars and epidemics. She credited her survival to God and luck and her sanity to her preoccupation with intellectual things. Melba was certain that ideas could be trusted. She had no such certainty about people.

Melba was at the top of her intellectual game by the time the digital technologies began the grand transformation of Africa. She knew history, politics, a lot of the sciences and was a whiz at using technology. She had been a major force in bringing mobile phones to Mozambique and in making certain the mobile devices in her country continued to be upgraded as the technology became available. She was often referred to in the press as Mobile Mama Melba.

Before the walking tour of Stone Town had ended, Melba was determined to hire Vasco Meghiji for the AllAfricaWiki. She felt certain it was a step that would lead to useful outcomes for both Vasco and the wiki. For Vasco it would mean the base for the next several years of his education. For the wiki, she predicted, it would develop a superior talent as a historian of Africa.

119

Melba sent word to the wiki headquarters that she was extending her Stone Town stay. She asked Vasco if she could hire him as her personal guide for the next two days. He accepted eagerly and cleared the arrangement with his office, where they took 40% of the fee Melba paid and were delighted.

As Vasco showed Stone Town to Melba, she taught him how the truth of history emerges in the virtual world. "Vasco," she said many, many times, "just remember that the cloud is smart." The first time she said it he was deeply dubious. By the end of the second day Vasco knew she was right.

Vasco was fifteen when he signed on with AllAfricaWiki. Fifteen years later, in 2030, he was extensively knowledgeable on Zanzibar history and the Internet's undisputed authority on the emergence of accuracy in the cloud. "A great woman taught me that the cloud is smart," Vasco liked to say, "and don't you forget that."

The project that Melba had in mind for Vasco when she found him at age fifteen was the development of the virtual history of Stone Town as a model for emergent digital history. She was well aware that there were many different themes and threads through the history of Stone Town: ancient cultures, exotic spice trade, sojourning Europeans, preening sultans, secretive leopards and the 21st century story still unfolding of the African renewal.

Melba Muthemba was sure in her own mind that in 2015 there was no human individual who could present Stone Town history objectively. Vasca Meghiji had learned that hard lesson when the tour guides contradicted his grandfather. Melba said to her protégé: "Vasco, you start putting all the tales into the wiki and let things simmer. The true history of Stone Town will emerge."

And so it was that the Melba and Vasco showed the world how smart the cloud could be. Vasco began by writing up his grandfather's story and publishing it in the Stone Town section of the history of Zanzibar on the wiki. The next day Portuguese scholars began making edits. After a bit of a battle in the back channel the account of Portuguese travel through Stone Town stabilized.

A few edits were done over the months and years that followed, but not many. Melba observed to Vasco that history several hundred years old usually does not change much unless there is either a major new find, or a eager new scholar does some serious new digging. She pointed out that the discovery of Joseph's tomb in Egypt in 2028 had caused major new activity in many ancient study fields, but she said those types of discoveries are rare.

Over the months after he published the Portuguese account, Vasco wrote and published the thirteen other stories that he had originally gathered. There was one that couched the entire past thousand years of Zanzibar history as a denial of the rights of native people and animals. (Vasco knew there were no known aboriginal people of Zanzibar, but he credited the essay to his sources and pushed the "publish" button.) Vasco worked hard on the cloves story, adding every detail he could get from the local lore as well as the farmers of Zanzibar's prominence in clove agriculture. His history of the time and architecture of the sultans was detailed and richly illustrated.

While Vasco was adding substance to the Stone Town section of the wiki, Melba was contacting experts around the world on the subjects that were flowing into the section. Melba gave the experts editorial access and encouraged them to correct and add to what Vasco was producing. She created back channels so the experts could consult each other. As the years passed, Vasco found that seldom a week went by that he did not run across something new to add or something to correct in the Stone Town history section of AllAfricaWiki.

Notice began to be taken of the extensive descriptions of Stone Town history. Vasco realize that Stone Town was attracting a new kind of tourist: historians. As he worried about what to do for a career, he put together some things in his mind and decided that the historical tourist business could be profitable. During his twenties, he began with a bed and breakfast that his young wife helped run. They called it Gama Gables.

Two years after opening Gama Gables, with some investors from Mozambique that Melba introduced him to, Vasco developed the Stone Town History Villas project. A series of sultan era cottages were restored, each with a theme from history and culture such as Clove Cottage, Lisboa Lodge, Sultan Suites and Leopard Hideaway.

The interest of historians in Stone Town created a feedback loop through the cloud. The more that was published in the Stone Town history section of the AllAfricaWiki, the more research was stimulated. In 2026-27 a party of archeologists worked an excavation site north of Stone Town and discovered human skeletons that were older than the Great Pyramids of Egypt.

A controversy spread through historical circles—and through the Stone Town section online—over whether the bones belonged to ancient pirates or aborigines of Zanzibar. Vasco placed extensive materials about the dig into the wiki, including essays, interviews with the archeologists and images. In 2029 three more groups of archeologists started digging around Stone Town and Vasco established an archeology section for Stone Town in the wiki.

Through all of the online activity, experts in the fields involved learned from the material that grew and was modified in the wiki about Stone Town archeology, and corrected mistakes when they found them. When Vasco gave talks about his work with the wiki—which he often did both in Stone Town and when invited to lecture abroad—his favorite example of an online correction was the matter of the Sultan's Ring.

The Sultan's Ring was a name given, somewhat felicitously to a gold ring found in a crack between a floor and a wall in one of the 19th century houses that was restored in Stone Town in 2124. The ring was fairly small, not very heavy, contained no stones and was decorated only with a lightly etched pattern of leaves and flowers. When the workman who found it examined it his first thought was to call out, "Has anyone lost his wedding ring."

The Sultan's Ring became something of a mystery. It was displayed in the Stone Town Museum which was the pride of the city, located in the restored Dispensary. Vasco took pictures of the ring, including several close ups of the etched pattern, and published its story along with the images in the Stone Town history on the wiki. In 2026 he added a three-dimensional holograph of the ring.

The publication of the article about the ring at first caused a small flurry of speculation, but no one came up with an identification of its culture of origin or date. Vasco added a query box to the article about the Sultan's Ring, asking anyone who had information about it to post what they knew. Years went by and the cloud produced no information about the ring.

In March of 2030, the History Villas received a request to reserve the Sultan's Suites for a week in April. The reservation was made by the office of the Sultan of Oman. When the party of eleven checked into the suites, Vasco saw to it that the rooms contained baskets of local flowers to welcome the guests.

The next morning a man from the Oman's staff appeared at Vasco's office. He explained that the Sultan's daughter wanted a personal visit to see the Sultan's Ring at the museum. He said that the princess was thirteen-years-old and was adamant about seeing the ring in person. Secretly pleased with the request, Vasco arranged to escort the daughter himself to see the famed ring the next morning before the museum opened to the public.

The Oman staff man and the princess arrived by private car. The princess, dressed in expensive field clothes similar to those worn by archeologists, bounded up the dispensary stairs and shook Vasco's hand. "I want to be a historian like you," she exclaimed. Vasco smiled, as his worries about being able to deal with the princess began to subside.

Inside the museum they were joined by its director, who accompanied them to the glass case where the Sultan's Ring was exhibited. "How closely can I look at it," the princess asked.

"There is no harm in your handling it, I am sure," the director said. He unlocked the case and handed the ring to the princess. She looked it over carefully. She then pulled a magnifying glass out of her pocket and looked at it even more carefully.

"I thought so," she said beaming. As the three men watched she unbuttoned a pocket on her trousers and removed a small bag. Out of the bag she produced a ring that looked identical to the one in that had been in the case. "They are children's rings from the Sultan's court during the Stone Town days. I have six more of them."

The princess had seen the article about the Sultan's Ring when she was browsing the AllAfricaWiki on her mobile. She noticed that the ring look familiar and clicked the holograph tab. Up in front of her popped a three-dimensional replica of the ring that she could rotate and examine from every side. She felt sure the mystery ring was just another children's ring dropped by one of her ancestors who was playing in the room where it was found in Stone Town. No archeologist or historian had ever seen a sample of the rings because they were still being passed down through the sultans' families.

Whenever Vasco told the story of the Sultan's Ring in a talk, he would go on to say that after her discovery, he had arranged for the princess to become a junior editor at the AllAfricaWiki, which worked closely with historians on the Arabian Peninsula. And when he came to the end of the story he would say, "You see there that, as I said, the cloud is smart."

The Cloud Is Smart

The new way that knowledge is obtainable is a spectacular a change for human affairs. Before we could find it on the Internet, knowledge available for a subject like Stone Town of Zanzibar for most people was limited to a brief article in an encyclopedia. Experts for most any field of knowledge were separated by great distances and could seldom confer or edit each other's work. Someone in Africa who knew a lot about Stone Town not necessarily knew of a clove spice expert in India or England. Information modification and updating like that now done on a wiki could only happen among experts in the same room sitting around a table talking. Collaboration did happen now and then; a wiki is unending collaboration.

The the Internet started to get smart from its earliest days. Over the decade that began in the mid-1990s, knowledge from experts, universities, libraries, archives, laboratories and other brick and mortar knowledge spaces of the pre-digital age began trickling and then pouring on to the Internet where the knowledge took digital form. By the year 2000, a great deal of new knowledge could be found only on the Internet. No one, for example wanted to store on paper the information about genomes that was piling up; much of it only went into digital records. Publications like the Congressional Directory where changes were frequent stopped most printing and went online. Scientists put new discoveries online and published them in print later, if they got around to it.

As Dr. OO explained in the chapter on Content, ospheres formed for knowledge as it matured online. The ospheres interconnected and rich networks of what is known by humankind formed.

As massive waves of knowledge flowed into the Internet, perplexity grew over how to find, as Vasco worried: what is true? I can remember doing a search (in about 1997) for "George Washington" and having the top link returned by the search engine I used come back as a gas station in Georgia named "George Washington."

Then the guys who started Google found a way to emerge the link you are looking for. The reason Google is able to list the best links for what you are trying to find is because the cloud picks those links for you based on who has chosen them before. Nothing is yet known that can do the link selecting job as well. Google is tapping collective intelligence. In something of a fit of pique, Howard Rheingold explained it this way:

> These critiques insist that it's all-important to note that the individual is sovereign and mobs are dumb, but again they are looking through the wrong end of the telescope. Again, simplistic logic: Tell Google what commies they are. The page rank algorithm is a mob measure -- an aggregate of the linking decisions of many people. It works because the decisions are made by individuals who are acting in their self interest, trying to come up with relevant links for their web pages, but it works only because it aggregates those decisions. It isn't individual versus group -- it's a group made of individuals.[17]

A recent new wrinkle in collective intelligence has appeared. After mighty efforts by many bright people to organize the Internet, folksonomy is spontaneously capturing wisdom crowds. What happens is that you and I and all the other folks who use the cloud think of our own tags to identify our pieces of

---

17 SmartMobs.com. http://www.smartmobs.com/archive/2007/01/18/ninnys_who_conf....html

digital stuff. Folks (you and I) tag the smallest pieces of information and ideas as we use them, causing the material to organize itself and show up when you ask for it. Find a book on Amazon, dig out a photo in Flickr, find a shared interest on MySpace. In each, tags chosen by Internet users, just plain folks, will make your search smart.

The effect of the Internet cloud is to let us all be smart. More fundamentally, all those who connect to the Internet are what makes the cloud smart. It was the little princess from Oman who made the cloud smart about the Sultan's Ring when she added to the AllAfricaWiki article about it that it was a children's ring from the sultan days in Stone Town. Everyone who makes connections online contributes to the collective intelligence from which we all benefit.

The smartness of the cloud billows from the mixture of massive digital storage and the individual and collective intelligence that interact with stored and new knowledge online. Knowledge and its keepers and users intertwingle in the networked environment of the cloud. The new generation's future will find them becoming smarter through the knowledge that they hold in their hand. They already are.

DIY: Do It Yourself

Dr. OO Visits the Participatory Pantheon
March 2036

When we left Dr. OO at the end of the *Content* chapter story, he was lamenting to his wife, "It is so much more of a popular thing to be a social network butterfly. Content is definitely not king, but I remain its advocate."

Six months after that we join him as he is given a tour of Participatory Pantheon. His hostess and guide is the Honorary Leader of the Pantheon Directorate, Melba Muthemba of Mozambique. The Pantheon occupies the former world headquarters campus of what was once Asia's largest radio and television conglomerate. Nearby is the All Asia Spaceport which receives frequent traffic from the New Mexico Spaceport and other super speed landing facilities around the world. The Participatory Pantheon is visited by people—including crowds of kids on learning tours—from dozens of countries each year.

There are two parts to the Pantheon experience: The Past Pavilion and Participatory Pantheon. The Past Pavilion is a museum of pre-21st century media and communications. Now that the personal mobile has been the device ordinarily used to interact with the cloud and its Internet content for nearly two decades, children and the young adult generation have seldom seen configurations of wired together computer screens, keyboards and printers. The mobile has dominated communication for enough years that once ubiquitous machines such as the rotary dial telephone and the portable CD disk player are viewed as quaint.

As Melba rather quickly steered their visitor vehicle through the Past Pavilion, she said under her breath to Dr. OO, "Omar, we had a rotary phone in our house when I was a small child. They may be outdated, but quaint is going a little too far."

Dr. OO said, generously, "I had a Walkman CD music player when I was a child. They worked rather well, I would say."

"Absolutely," Melba said. "Let's hurry on to the Participatory Pantheon. I think you will be impressed. The Past Pavilion is really just there so the younger generations can understand its contrast with the new participatory trends that emerged in the first part of our new century."

The Participatory Pantheon is housed in a dome ten percent larger than the biggest football dome in the United States. The dome is a perfect circle—in fact a sphere that sits on the open Asian steppe with eighteen percent of the ball it forms beneath the level of the surrounding land. Inside the outer sphere is another perfect ball that is transparent. The inner ball is one half the size of the outer ball shell and is suspended in the exact middle of the inner space. The inner ball is known as the Intertwingularity.

Surrounding the Intertwingularity are visiting stations that are platforms next to the outer glass of the Intertwingularity. The visiting stations are spaced apart at various locations. They allow visitors who are standing on them to see into the entire inner space of the Intertwingularity. The visitors stations are named for different kinds of participatory activity that affect the Intertwingularity. The names are: Blogging, Wikis, Smart Mobbing, Folksonomy, Music Mashup, Viral Videoing, Gaming, Mobile Photography, Locationing—and at least five more names which anyone writing in 2007 could not possibly anticipate.

When Melba and Dr. OO first entered the Participatory Pantheon, she guided their visitor vehicle to a cog clip that lifted them to a high overview of the Intertwingularity. The two sat for a few minutes simply taking in the beautiful complexity. Inside of the great glass ball there is incalculable activity. At every imaginable angle there are patterns of static connections of tiny lines of light. There are innumerable pinpoints of light. Flowing, dashing, sparking and blinking among the areas that seem static is a great deal more connecting and disconnecting. Clusters of the light within the seeming chaos abound—many sizes of clusters with a few very large ones.

Finally, Dr. OO said to Melba, "All of that represents something real, doesn't it?"

"Yes," she said, "Our engineers tell me it may show us as much as two one thousandths of one percent of a piece of the cloud. And some of it, Omar, is those ospheres of content you like to talk about."

"Wonderful!" he said. "Which parts."

Melba described how some of the content, such as the information displayed from the servers of a museum expert's website is essentially static. "That kind of material," she said, "sits there like a little network—or piece of osphere as you would say—so that someone who comes to learn from it just goes in and out like to moving flashes we are watching."

"And the osphere for a subject like ancient Greek sculpture would be the small network within that museum plus its links out from the small network to all the other sources in the Intertwingularity about ancient Greek Sculpture," Dr. OO, warming up to his speaking cadence used in lectures added eagerly, "Can I see an osphere in there?"

Melba showed him how to find the Participatory Pantheon control panel on his mobile. She said she recalled that Greek Art was one of the subjects in the demonstration suite for the Pantheon. Dr. OO located Greek Art on the list and clicked "ancient sculpture" in the subtopics. His mobile sent a visible stream of light toward the great transparent ball.

A pattern of about fifty pinpoints of light intensified and then links among them began to grow. As Dr. OO pointed his mobile at different points of light, labels appeared on his mobile screen giving names of museums, private collectors and archeological sites.

Melba said, "Your osphere pattern there is pretty much static. The Pantheon is more about what happens when we human interact with the cloud—when we participate in aggregation and creation."

They were silent again for a full three minutes. Then Dr. OO spoke: "I want to try the participatory thing."

"Which one?" Melba asked, "how about blogging?"

"Tell me about my choices, if you would," he said, sounding thoroughly uncertain.

"Maybe we should just try one first," she said. "It will make more sense then." She pushed the release from the cog that was holding the visitor vehicle and they slid down a track, then back up again, to find themselves on the Mobile Photography visitor station. Melba then asked Dr. OO, "Have you got a photo you think might get a reaction out of the Intertwingularity?"

Dr. OO began fumbling with his mobile as he looked through his Flickr archive. Melba watched him with a twinkle in her eye. She knew he is a photographer and that he had contributed some images of Irish fish to scientific and sports collections. As she guessed, he soon suggested that an image he had of a very large trout might be worth a launch. She then told him to pick some key words with which to tag the fish.

Dr. OO followed her instructions as he prepared a digital message that included the image of the fish and the word tags: trout, record, 2013, Lough_Corrib, Ireland. He beamed the message from his mobile to the visitor station input port to the Intertwingularity. Above the input port a sign read: "Your input activity will be purple."

As he tried to count them about thirty purple flashes bounced here and there inside the great glass ball. In less than a second a message appeared on his mobile screen and on the large output banner of the Mobile Photography visitor station. It read: "Larger trout caught in 2013 in Lough Inagh, Ireland. Your image is likely not to be very active."

Dr. OO blushed as Melba laughed. "A fisherman is allowed to exaggerate," he said sheepishly.

"Not when you participate in the Intertwingularity. Remember, the cloud is smart." she said.

Next they visited the Blogging visitors station where you can select a blogger's stream of posts to flow into the Intertwingularity. Dr. OO picked a favorite political blogger and turned the switch on. A flow of turquoise dashes began moving into the Intertwingularity. Each one morphed into a pattern of connections to pinpoints of light, and then some of the pinpoints interconnected with each other. Melba pointed out that one of the dashes—representing a new post just put on the blog—must have been on a particularly explosive topic because it seemed to bounce all over the giant ball before things calmed down.

At the Locationing visitors station, Dr. OO was able to create patterns in the Intertwingularity by entering the mobile numbers of people on his contact list. The locations where those people happened to be was tracked through the Interwingularity into the full Internet cloud, and made visible as pinpoints inside the great ball.

The Smart Mobbing visitor station is located near the Locationing station. A mobbing map panel allows the visitor to zoom in on a square mile section of any place on earth, and then to attempt to send a mob of dots to that area—virtually, of course. Real people are not used for the demonstration of smart mobs. Dr. OO tried three times to mob the offices of sporting officials in Dublin with football fans demanding safer seating at the Croke Park stadium. In the third attempt the mob got so large it trampled eight bystanders. Dr. OO told Melba he needed to learn more about how to make a mob smart enough not to do that.

At the Music Mash-up visitors station, Dr. OO connected to a drummer friend in Dublin, who input some trills. At the Dublin drummer's suggestion they added a flutist in France and a cellist in Czechoslovakia. The Intertwingularity responded to the triple input with a joyous small light show and then output a mashed-up melody into the mobiles of all concerned.

After he tried the participation techniques at most of the stations, Melba took Dr. OO to the Wiki visiting station last. She explained that her work with AllAfricaWiki had been her introduction to participatory online methods and that it had made her a true believer. She said to Dr. OO, "I know you are an advocate of straight content: just have the experts put the knowledge on a server and depend on their reputation for its authenticity. But I have come to believe that when everyone who cares about a subject can participate in keeping it available for everyone else, that is a good thing."

Dr. OO had no argument. He nodded and said, "You have made a believer of me, Melba. How can I say anything? My information about the trout was wrong. Somebody else knew there was a bigger fish caught at Lough Inagh. The Intertwingularity didn't know by itself. Someone out here told them: the power of the Participatory Pantheon is everybody."

Melba backed the visitor vehicle once again into a cog track that lifted them to the overall observation level. When they were parked, Melba said, "Now for the People Pattern, Omar, this is the most beautiful, and important, of all." She pointed her mobile at a large white statue of the Greek god Zeus that stood at the very top of the great glass ball. Melba sent a beam toward Zeus. When the signal she sent hit him, he reached back and then hurled a lightning bolt at the great glass ball on which he was standing.

The lightning bolt hit and went through the glass shell of the ball. When it was inside, the lightning's visible energy spread throughout the space within ball creating a massive warm brown network of connections that integrated into all of the other pinpoints and connectivity. "There is your social networking, Omar. The warm brown network is human beings connecting to each other and to the wikis, blogs, music, images—and everything else. Everything that happens within the Intertwingularity can be traced back to the ideas and actions of individual people. Everything emerges from how all of that networks: knowledge, ideas, actions and people—how it all intertwingles."

Thus, as he told his wife when he got home, Omar O'Malley began to realize that social networking has a lot to be said for it. He also told his wife that the Intertwingularity had caught him exaggerating about a fish. She said, "Druid, I suspect you were just testing to see if the cloud was smart enough to catch you," to which he did not reply.

DIY: Participatory Intertwingularity

The odds are not too great that by 2036 there will be a giant glass ball suspended inside an even larger ball that sits in the middle of Asia and is visited by people from all parts of the world so they can interact with a visualization of collective intelligence and participatory creativity within the Internet.. Moving on from that whimsy, though, the fact is that everything else described in the Participatory Pantheon story is happening now. It is perfectly legitimate to think of the cloud as the Intertwingularity. In it—whatever we call it—there is a massive human (social) network of activity that includes participation in these activities: blogging, wikis, smart mobbing, folksonomy, music mash-ups, viral videoing, gaming, mobile photography and locationing.

The digital cloud that has engulfed our planet and the Internet of communication and content within it are, for sure, a great big ball of complexity. Thinking of that big ball as the Intertwingularity helps me to understand that everything is interconnected—and that those interconnections are interactive and far more rich and diverse than simple hierarchies, categories and sequences.

Some of the stuff that intertwingles in the big ball—the cloud—is content of the sort that in the past we have kept in libraries, archives and the heads of experts.

Much of the intertwingling action consists of social networking—of people connecting to each other. In the cloud, because it is a network environment, people can interconnect and interact beyond the simple receiving of broadcast information or the two-way conversations that dominated the telephone era.

A third sort of intertwingularity—that has become the subject of much inquiry and discussion in the times in which I write this book—is called participatory or DIY ("do it yourself"). In the story of the Participatory Pantheon I have tried to introduce this many faceted subject which is, simply put, you, me and everybody else making things happen online. Everybody else includes a high proportion of the youngest generation.

The wiki is an early example of participatory methods. Wiki is defined by Wikipedia's Wiktionary as: *A collaborative website which can be directly edited by anyone with access to it.*[18] As an example of how a wiki works, Vasco in the Cloud Is Smart story was determined to see the history of Stone Town correctly stated on the AllAfricaWiki. When Vasco found something new to add or something to correct he would do it himself—thus DIY. He simply went online into the Stone Town history section and changed what the AllAfricaWiki said. If someone else had better information, he or she would do the same, as the princess did with the children's ring, once again updating and refining the history. Participatory editing kept the section up to speed with everything interested people knew about the history of Stone Town.

Wikipedia is the great early example of participatory editing. The project explains itself with this introduction:

> Since its creation in 2001, Wikipedia has rapidly grown into the largest reference Web site on the Internet. The content of Wikipedia is free, and is written collaboratively by people from all around the world. This Web site is a wiki, which means that anyone with access to an

---

18   Wiktionary, January 26, 2007. http://en.wiktionary.org/wiki/wiki

Internet-connected computer can edit, correct, or improve information throughout the encyclopedia, simply by clicking the edit this page link (with a few minor exceptions, such as protected articles and the main page).[19]

Wikipedia was founded by Jimmy Wales, who has continued to lead the undertaking. In an interview published on iCommons.org late in 2006, Wales' answers to questions state great strengths of participatory online media:

>   *Question:* How have you managed to protect Wikipedia from vandalism, while still fostering openness and accessibility?

>   *Wales:* Wiki software contains many controls whereby the community is able to quickly revert vandalism. But as it turns out, most people are good, and the vulnerability of a wiki is its own best protection mechanism. It isn't much of a challenge to vandalize a wiki page, but someone fixes it a moment later, so there is nothing much fun about doing that.

>   *Question:* What has Wikipedia taught you about human nature?

>   *Wales:* People are much nicer than I ever knew.[20]

Wikipedia was an early major player in a participatory online phenomenon that rumbled through the Napster wars and emerged into powerful prominence with the explosion of blogging and the huge growth of happenings like American Idol, MySpace and YouTube. All of these, and many knock-offs and copy cats, are based on participation. A nickname for these activities is DIY, "do it yourself."

Henry Jenkins, founder and director of the Comparative Media Studies Program at MIT described DIY activities in terms of cultural creation in remarks to the USC Annenberg Center DIY seminar:

>   "Amateur content is getting global visibility. And fan communities are not just distribution channels, but the seedbeds of cultural creation," Jenkins stated, in a kind of "ecological relationship with blogs and grass-

---

19   Wikipedia: About. January 26, 2007. http://en.wikipedia.org/wiki/Wikipedia:About
20   iCommons.org, December 2006. http://icommons.org/2006/12/page/2/

133

roots communities that create cultural material and social networks that distribute it."[21]

There is no way to overstate how complex these mechanisms are. On top of that, we do not yet understand very well what is going on in the digital cloud as it clearly is playing a significant role in shaping the future. I have only touched on some high points.

In calling this chapter DIY, I have revealed my own inclination—like that of Dr. OO—to put the individual and expert content first. Another good word for the participation phenomena is collaboration, which is a contribution of social networking and the emphasis on it that is preferred by some. I have fallen in love with the word intertwingle because it is without bias for DIY or social networking; it perfectly names both.

You may have thought through these pages that I have relied too heavily on the word intertwingle, and perhaps I have. But what other word is there to describe the synergy of individual action, content, social networking and participation we have been exploring? For the new generation, using mobile phones they already do, heavily involves them in this synergy. It is an important part of their lives now. To understand their future, why not view their new virtual synergy as a Pantheon of light and enlightenment where they intertwingle freely and have the liberty through their lives participate as they choose?

---

21   DIY Media Weblog, January 24, 2007. http://weblogs.annenberg.edu/diy/2007/01/henry_jenkins_at_diy_media_sem_1.html

LEARNING
Why education must and will intertwingle very soon

A Perfect Storm

Fanatical Auntie Blanche
October 2030

"The whole world hates a pushy broad," Alice thought to herself as she stared at her shouting Auntie Blanche projected on the uniscreen at the back of her desk. Now forty-six-years-old, Councilwoman Blanche is without a doubt New York City's most vocal advocate for digital rights. Her niece Alice, fifteen years younger than Blanche, greatly respects her Aunt's dedication, but is often embarrassed by how outspoken she is.

As Alice slumped down in her chair to watch her shouting aunt on the screen, she began getting angry. The dear old former Mayor, now nearly ninety, was sitting in the row of dignitaries behind Auntie Blanche as she railed away at how his administration had forbidden the children of New York to have mobiles with them at school.

Suddenly Alice's anger turned to embarrassment as Auntie Blanche started talking about her saying, "My niece Alice is a perfect example of why children needed to be mobile-equipped back then. The mobiles saved Alice's life at least twice, once physically and once intellectually."

"Of course what she says is true," Alice thought to herself, "but Auntie Blanche is still fighting battles from long ago. I don't think she understands yet that people my age now not only use mobiles—much of our lives are shaped and greatly improved by them."

The people of the City of New York had often before heard Council-woman Blanche's two stories about mobiles saving her niece Alice. The first story made it into the police records and is well established fact. On October 18, 2007, then seven-year-old Alice was walking to school on a cloudy and dark morning. As she walked past a dumpster a man moved quickly from behind it on to the sidewalk to block her route. He smiled warmly and said he was hungry.

Alice always recalled the incident with quite a bit of fear, but with some pride too. Years later she remembers clearly that she did not believe the man for one second. She looked up at him and said she had an apple in her lunch pack. Before he had time to react, she reached into her pack, pushed the alarm button on her mobile that was inside the pack on the bottom, and swiftly pull out the apple. She pushed herself to smile, handing him the apple. He took it, and then offered to drive her to school. She followed him, jumping through the door he

137

opened into the car parked in front of the dumpster.

The mobile alarm sent a signal to the phones of her father, mother and to the main administrative computer at the school. As the car drove away, Alice set her pack next to her on the seat. The locator signal from the mobile inside the pack was picked up immediately by the police, when the calls came in from her parents and school. As Alice sat with her hands in her lap trying not to look frightened, the man turned the car away from the direction of the school. She kept remembering she had sent the alarm and tried to be brave.

The police records show that the man was apprehended within fifteen minutes of the time the alarm was sent by Alice. She remembered that they were driving down a street she did not recognize when the man suddenly stopped the car, jumped out and started running away. She peeked over the dashboard and it looked like there were police everywhere. She saw that several of them had grabbed the man and he was kicking.

On Alice's uniscreen, Auntie Blanche was going on and on about how even if her little niece had not pushed the alarm the mobile would have protected her in other ways. If she had been late to school her route and whereabouts could be tracked.

Although Alice has remained grateful for the protection her mobile gave her as a small child, what her Auntie Blanche calls the second big mobile thing seems at least as important. Now a private teacher of biology with students as young as eight-years and old as mid-teens, Alice finds it hard to imagine acquainting young people with what were once thought of as school subjects without letting them use their mobiles.

One of the three locations where Alice teaches is the former Queens middle school library where she is sitting watching her Auntie Blanche rant on the uniscreen mounted on the central desk in the large room. A uniscreen is built into each of the tables scattered through the room. Students can look at incoming digital material on the small screen of their own mobile by projecting a haloscreen in front of them, or by sending the image to a uniscreen.

By the time Alice is watching Auntie Blanche, in the year 2030, how young people learn and are taught has been reinvented, with the individual student's mobile the core means for retrieving and interfacing knowledge as well as a tool of interaction among learners and teachers. Alice felt very lucky to be one of the new professional teachers of 21st century education. She thought to herself that her own escape from the kind of education they put up with in the twentieth century was at least as important as how she had fooled that man who tried to abduct her in his car. Twentieth century education probably would have succeeded in abusing her mind.

A Perfect Storm

Before the day comes when everyone begins working together to make certain every young person has a mobile that interacts with the cloud for learning, some say the education establishment will be battered by a convergence worthy to be called a perfect storm. In the late spring of 2006, I observed a startling warning sign of such a perfect storm slamming traditional education. The event I witnessed happened in the same middle school library where Alice will one day teach. The following is the account of that actual event.

I was at the middle school library as one of a group of four judges of a *Project Citizen* competition. We observed the presentations of two teams of seventh graders proposing and supporting changes in public policy.

The second team we judged advocated the end of random scanner searches at schools. The team began their presentation with a skit in which five of the kids played the role of students and one was a security man. The team had built a walk-through cardboard frame and model hand scanner. One-by-one the kids playing students walked through the frame and were then searched by the security man who passed his hand scanner up and down their bodies. Every search located a cell phone that the guard took from the student. The students acted disgusted as their phones were taken, but did not resist. Following the skit, the team argued passionately that they should be allowed to keep their phones and against the claim of the largest school district on earth that it had a right to take their phones away.

One of the student speakers said that the guards with scanners would confiscate "box cutters, guns, knives, electronics, and cell phones." A newspaper article at the time reported that the authorities had confiscated 36 weapons, mostly knives, since scanning started — and 3,027 cellphones."[22]

Why are mobile phones on the same list with lethal weapons? A New York City Council hearing was held about the confiscations on the evening of the day I did the judging. The New York Times reported that at that meeting:

> Administrative officials, backed by a panel of three principals, defended the ban, saying that students have used phones to cheat on exams, summon friends for fights, take illicit locker-room photographs

---

22   Elissa Gootman. School Phone Ban Stirs, Yes, a Lot of Talk, New York Times, June 15, 2006

of classmates and disrupt class.

"The reality is that if cellphones are allowed in our schools, they will be used, and they will be used inappropriately," said Deputy Mayor Dennis M. Walcott.[23]

The two classes of seventh graders gathered in the library for the competition for which I was a judge were a mixture of many national and ethnic backgrounds. The youngsters were all polite and well-behaved. Some of the speakers were poised and articulate while others were less effective. Every one of them showed heat when advocating his or her right to carry a phone. The students argued that the cell phone ban infringed their rights and that the phones have become an important safety factor for children. I think what they cared about most deeply was their rights.

One of the judges on the panel of which I was a member was a highly respected teacher recently retired after thirty-four years on the faculty of a large Brooklyn High School. She was renowned as a speaking coach whose students had filled shelves at her school with significant major trophies from forensics competition. Rising to the occasion in the middle school, she carefully challenged the kids we were judging to think about what they were saying. She then took the idea that Deputy Mayor Walcott used to draw a line in the sand. Like the Deputy Mayor, she said the phones interfere with education.

One of the girls on the team came right back at this judge, disagreeing. After a couple of exchanges between the young girl and veteran teacher, the teacher said, "Which would you choose, your phone or your education?" The girl looked startled and then answered from her heart, I believe, when she said, "My phone." The judges and the kids were all a bit taken aback, and the subject was changed.

That girl that looked established education in the eye and said, "My phone," is my inspiration for Auntie Blanche.

Five months after the confrontation in the middle school library in Queens, I wrote the following post for SmartMobs.com, Howard Rheingold's blog where I am a member of the writing team:

Education's the perfect storm rumbles in New York City
Here in New York City we have the world's largest public school system. It was taken over by Mayor Bloomberg when he was elected to

---

23   Ibid.

his first term. Our kids, like everyone else's around the world, have cell phones. The Mayor does too, yet for youngsters he makes no connection between mobiles and improving education. So we have this sound bite—putting kids down—today from Mayor Bloomberg on WCBS New Radio 880, recorded by reporter Rich Lamb:

Lamb: Hearing that some New York City public school students are smuggling cell phones into classrooms in their underwear or in hollowed out calculators, Mayor Bloomberg concluded that if the kids would put half that effort into improving their education they would be better off.
Mayor: There is nothing wrong with cell phones. I carry one. There is nothing wrong with iPods. I have two, as a matter of fact. But they just don't belong in the classroom. Our teachers have enough to do without policing the use of electronic devices.
Lamb: The mayor says if you have them you are going to have them on, and if you have them on they are going to disrupt other people.[24]

An obvious indication that the kids will keep their cell phones is the fact that it is happening. On the sad day in October 2006 when Yankee baseball pitcher Cory Lidle's small airplane hit a New York City apartment building, the New York Times coverage included this eyewitness report by a New York City public school student:

Samuel Klotman, 17, was on the roof of his school nearby with classmates when they saw the plane coming down.
"I could see through the buildings what I thought was a plane headed to this building," he said. "Then there was a booming noise and a great fire gust shooting out."
He said he and his classmates started text messaging and calling everyone they knew, "wondering what was happening," and the school let everybody go home.[25]

In Manhattan, the roof of a school is part of the school, usually a playground or sports area. Students standing on a school roof are at school and

24   http://www.smartmobs.com/archive/2006/11/17/educations_the_....html
25   http://www.nytimes.com/2006/10/11/nyregion/12crashcnd.html?hp&ex=1160625600&en=43676d689354db2c&ei=5094&partner=homepage

thereby in violation of the Mayor's mandate if they have mobile phones with them. The disconnect between reality and official school policy in these reports is laughable.

The situation is not unique to New York City. A nine-year-old I interviewed who attends a public elementary school in suburban Cincinnati told me that if anyone is caught with a phone in school "they are in big trouble." A friend in Texas asked her grandsons who attend high school if they were allowed to have mobile phones with them in school. She reported that they each told her of incidences where they were in violation of the rule not to have phones available when their mobile "fell out" in class. The boys noted to their grandmother that when this rather difficult to visualize event of a phone "falling out" occurred for each of them, the one who made better grades got in less trouble than the one who was not as good a student. A blogger who writes in the UK about mobiles commented in spring 2006 that his daughter was complaining because her school was tightening mobile restrictions at exam time.

In the relative quite before the perfect storm that is headed toward education, the main public arguments in favor of letting kids carry phones to school are safety and convenience. The story of Alice and the man who picked her up points to the growing trend for small children to carry phones as a way for parents to know where they are and for children to be able to call for assistance. Older kids and their parents argue that the phones are necessary to keep in touch and for teenagers to be responsible to jobs and other obligations.

Certainly the main reason youngsters want the phones is because they have become more and more a part of the lifestyle of children and adolescents. It is through this fundamental new way of doing things that the mobiles are a key part of what will soon knock traditional education off of its foundations. How young people learn will begin again in radically new ways.

Calling what is brewing for education "a perfect storm" picks up a term used by Adjunct Professor, in the Interactive Media Division of the USC School of Cinema-Television, Todd Richmond in a presentation he made as a Fellow at the USC Annenberg Center and the Center for Creative Technologies at USC. The following quotation is from a post on the DIY Media Weblog by Howard Rheingold reporting what Richmond said:

> With Wi-Fi in the classroom and lecture videos online, and student familiarity with laptops, remix, mashups, blogs and wikis, together with the power that "Googlepedia" teachers and learners, the delta in education is changing: the previously strictly hierarchical relationships

between teacher and learner are changing.

"Resistance is futile," believes Richmond: although existing educational institutions are not generally embracing a digitally transformed future, "the educational sector will be dragged into the future kicking and screaming by the next perfect storm."[26]

A key reason the education sector will not be able to withstand the coming storm is the declining stock placed by the public in the lines of defense the education establishment has trotted out over and over. Through most of the time that digital innovation was revolutionizing other sectors, a continuing slippage for education into mediocrity has taken place around a set of usual excuses for its failure: more money is needed, the students do not get what they need at home and problems are social, not about how teaching and learning are done—the education establishment is the victim not the cause.

In November 2006 I attended *Innovation & Growth in a Flat World*, a leadership panel chaired by David Kirkpatrick, Internet Technology senior Editor of Fortune, with panelists New York Times columnist Thomas Friedman, publisher Tim O'Reilly, CollabNet founder and CTO Brian Behlendorf and Reuters COO David Wenig. The audience that filled the hotel ballroom in New York's Times Square were business men and women. The occasion was sponsored by CollabNet as a treat for this executive gathering to hear a top panel discuss the future of business in our newly flat world — a phrase coined by Thomas Friedman. Also to be discussed was Web 2.0 — a phrase defined by Tim O'Reilly.

In the most hopeful sign I have yet seen that education will soon be forced to confront new reasons for change—to become part of the flat world that is characterized by Web 2.0—the question and answer exchange with the audience spontaneously turned away from business to the subject of education. In a change from what has been routine in the past, the discussion did not protect established education with the usual excuses.

Brian Behlendorf talked about a recent paper by John Seely Brown that described a college classroom in which screens were placed around the room to display what students were doing with their laptops. David Kirkpatrick agonized that not much is really being done about bringing K-12 into the online era. Tim O'Reilly pointed out that credentialing is moving toward "what have you built?" and away from "what school did you graduate from?" Tom Friedman described

---

26   DYI Media Weblog. http://weblogs.annenberg.edu/diy/2006/10/todd_richmond_on_open_educatio.html

completely revising his take on education, using a different set of quotients, in the new edition of his best-selling book *The World Is Flat*.

The old clichés about needing to pour more money into education, kids coming from bad homes etc. did not come up. The panel looked to the new connected world instead for answers to education's woes.

The future where everyone has a mobile described in this book operates on the factors that are making the world flat, as Friedman calls it, by the implementation of Web 2.0, as O'Reilly describes. They are background for understanding the kind of world that will emerge after the perfect storm is over—when the education we have known for the past couple of centuries is blown down and away.

Todd Richmond said that "the educational sector will be dragged into the future kicking and screaming by the next perfect storm." I think there will, in fact, be a starting over: the education sector itself will recede. When that happens, the ground can be cleared for new foundations and structures of learning for youngsters into the increasingly digitally transformed future. The impending perfect storm will thus save time in getting to the exciting and promising work of engaging knowledge in grand new ways. Huge efforts are being made today to save the schools—effort that is increasingly more obviously a waste. When we are able to let go of backward visions of schools, it will be much easier to focus on seeing to it that our children are learning. In this scenario, traditional education is obsolete and the digital storm removes its debris.

These dire predictions of sector smashing are not at all exaggerated. What a perfect storm would do to education fits a broad pattern of sector smashing in the digital transformations of recent years. Take the vaunted secretarial segment of the professional and business sectors of the 20th century. To be elevated to having a private office and a desk with a buzzer that summoned a secretary was once a widely coveted symbol of success. But the order to, "Take a letter Miss Jones," is obsolete, and so of course is calling her, "Miss." The intelligent, hard-working women who used to respond to the buzzers were not elevated by feminism. They were made obsolete and fired because of the desktop computer and, more recently, her boss's mobile that provides many of the services she once did. The secretaries went home or learned a new career.

Another pleasant and profitable type of business and occupation that was decimated early on in the digital transformation was the travel agent. Even before the Internet made it possible for passengers to select and buy tickets online, big computers took over the scheduling and tracking of airplanes, ships and trains, replacing human agents at many levels of the process.

144

The occupational world of advertising has been in upheaval since the first digital imaging began flooding the print side. Television production of all sorts was lifted from its linear restraints by digital editing while the advertising profit side was dealt staggering body blows from remote mutes and Tivo—leading to the digital phoenix now rising of advertising in the cloud. Audio tapes have succumbed to CDs and rental movie tapes are withering in the hurricane of DVDs. The perfect storm that hit the music industry began with early squalls of downloads from desktop computers and howled into full fury when Napster came ashore, spawning iPods, iTunes and creating a still emerging new musicosphere.

Yet through it all, nearly all K-12 classrooms remain firewalled and the textbook has changed very little except to become fatter, heavier and more expensive. Since the chatter began about the information highway and the buzz was growing louder about the Internet, it has been assumed by the schools that they would choose and control what digital knowledge was allowed inside their ivy walls. It would be educators who would determine when and how students would interact with the new virtual world. Very little interaction has been allowed, especially before young people arrive at college.

The ability to maintain the assumption that the powers of education determine digital interaction changes completely when the students have the digital world in their pockets. As we have seen above, the general reaction of the education establishment to the devices has been to forbid kids to bring the mobiles they already own into the classroom—or even to let them fall out of their pockets.

Even so, many education watchers say with justifiable skepticism: what will make things change for education happen now, when the establishment has been so successful thus far in keeping the digital innovations at arms length? The genius of Dr. Richmond's prediction is the concept of "perfect storm," which Wikipedia defines:

> The phrase perfect storm refers to the simultaneous occurrence of events which, taken individually, would be far less powerful than the result of their chance combination. Such occurrences are rare by their very nature, so that even a slight change in any one event contributing to the perfect storm would lessen its overall impact.[27]

The simultaneous occurrence of events that will clear the educational landscape will not occur in the classroom. It is happening in the virtual world

27   http://en.wikipedia.org/wiki/Perfect_storm

to which kids already connect, with increasing richness as each month passes, through the mobiles in their pockets. Before the end of the first 21st century decade, this synergy that is outside of education's ivy walls will make the classroom essentially obsolete for engaging prime knowledge because that knowledge will be digital, openly available online and accessible through mobile devices. It will be in the students' pockets, not in printed textbooks or instructors' heads.

Whirling through the gusts of the impending perfect storm are factors named by Dr. Richmond: Wi-Fi, lecture videos online, laptops, remix, mashups, blogs and wikis, and "Googlepedia." All of these are outside of the classroom, and outside of established education itself. There are, in fact, over ten years of innovations for knowledge, thinking and creativity abounding in the online world that education has barely picked at and never embraced.

The new ways to engage knowledge leave textbooks, wall charts, pen and chalk behind. These changes elevate the teacher to a professional, morphing pedagogue into Socrates. Pedagogue means to lead a child to knowledge. Socrates told students to go find the knowledge and then come to discourse with him. The online world offers human teachers a Socratic role like Alice has in 2030, in a room that was once the library of a middle school—where her Auntie Blanche chose her phone over the education she was receiving in 2006.

Unschooling

Euclid Eastliman Interviewed by an African Reporter
June 2030

Euclid: "Well, I just rode the first curve. I was very, very lucky. Mother was a single mom, with three of us. I was the youngest, born the day the new century began. I even got my picture in the Daily News! There I am, a wrinkled black mug peeking out of a blanket, with Daddy grinning and giving the camera a huge wink.

"Mother has told me that Daddy thought it was the funniest possible co-incidence that a bad man like him won all those prizes because his kid was the first one born in that hospital in the twenty-first century. He had been dealing drugs for years, and was shot dead by an opposing gang when I was three. I have no real memory of the man, but they say he was very intelligent. Good genes, bad morals I guess."

"Dad had always dropped by now and then to give Mother rent and food money—and a nice gift every time he came. When he died, she went to work on a building cleaning crew in Lower Manhattan. She worked hard and is a smart lady. Before long she was supervising a floor crew in the new Liberty Tower. That turned out to be a very lucky move for me."

"We had been living in a housing project in Manhattan—in South Harlem. Everybody that lived there was black. The old public school was still the first place we little kids got into the bigger world. At least that was what we thought it was. In any event, when Mother first got promoted to supervisor, in 2008, we moved to Battery Park City where the neighborhood was mixed.

"But my big break was the Liberty Unschooling Project where Mother got me enrolled in 2009. She had been working hard at home to get me up to speed on skills: reading, writing, arithmetic. My older siblings, both sisters, had me tapping text into their mobiles before I was five. But dear old 'LUP,' as we kids called Liberty Tower's unschooling project, is where my brain got in gear."

"The motto at LUP, which as you may know thrives today at the Liberty Tower and has been copied in many places around the world, is 'The rich get richer.' Of course that phrase is from network theory. When it becomes the mantra for small children, they learn to get really good where their natural talents are and at doing thing that attract their interests.

"For me, I realized very early at LUP that I was born to be a lawyer and that I could become very good at that. By the second year that I was in LUP, when

147

I was ten-years-old, I had been assigned to the famed Wimberly, Swan, Burtis & Alexander law firm whose offices occupied the seventieth through seventy-fourth floors of Liberty Tower. It sounds perhaps silly to say that some of the lawyers there came to be like uncles and aunts to me. But when you are ten-years-old and meet people who are trying to nurture and teach you, that is what they feel like. I still call Mr. Burtis, who is now in his nineties, 'Uncle B.' Happily I get to see him several times a year because we are both on the LUP Advisors Board and we both are very faithful about attending meetings. I can't think of anything more important that I do than supporting LUP.

"Although the LUP format has been tinkered with over the years, it still is based on dividing kids' participation into three areas. They are instructed and equipped in using digital devices for accessing and learning the knowledge of humankind. They are supported in activities where they develop their choices for expression, including visual and performing arts, speaking, negotiation and sports. They are assigned to a mentoring and apprenticing venue in the adult world.

"As an enrolled Luppie, a youngster chooses to spend as much time as he or she would like in any of the three areas, or—and this is very important—to spend time doing none of the three. That is the unschooling aspect of LUP. Goofing off, playing, chatting with friends or just staring into space are permitted and even encouraged.

"The part that usually surprises people is that discipline is self-imposed. Well, I do not think that should be a surprise. The LUP Honor Code is not complicated. Religions have called it the Golden Rule: Do unto others as you would have them do unto you. And as you might imagine, enforcing that is one of the major challenges at LUP. I believe it was that challenge which drew me into my decision to become an attorney.

"From the time I was eleven, I was a member of the Honors Task Force. We worked hard to keep the enforcement of the Honor Code in the hands of the Luppies and not the adults. To do that we had an Honors Court and Luppie lawyers as young as ten representing Luppies who had been accused of infractions. Sometimes we asked lawyers from our mentoring firm to sit in on panels. The challenge turned out to be like the real world judiciary: never perfectly solved.

INTERVIEWER: "When did you graduate from LUP?"

Euclid: "LUP is unschooling, remember. So there is ungraduating, as we like to call it. Luppies leave whenever they choose, often around the age of sixteen. That is what I did, because by then Columbia Law School had quit giving grades and granted my request to sit as a law reader there for a year.

"The CLS Reader Program allowed those of us who were in it to sit in on lectures by the faculty. I was blown away by that experience. The exchange between the young, bright questioners and the grizzled experts was stimulating, subtle and great thinking exercise. Since the class attendees older than I was, who were already applying for law firm jobs and clerkships, did not have to worry about being graded, they would ask the professors about ideas that puzzled them. Sometimes the professor would launch into an analysis of the issue that was brought up in the question. Just as often the professor would fiddle around with her mobile and then point it at us and beam over a reading list. She would tell us to read what the writers on the list had to say and then promised a discussion of the issue in a future class. And I suppose I shouldn't have implied that the female professors were grizzled, but frankly, some of them were.

INTERVIEWER: "If I can ask a candid question . . .

Euclid: "Of course."

INTERVIEWER: "Being black, I suppose you had all kinds of law firm job offers by the time you were twenty-years-old?"

Euclid: "Funny you should ask. Getting hired by a top law firm was a lot harder for blacks by the time I was the right age to come into a firm as an associate. There has been a complete flip since the early part of the century. Now as a black lawyer you have to compete with the smartest black men and women, as well, of course with the cream of the whites, Asians and the rest. Once the school system holding them back broke down, those black kids came on like gangbusters, as the saying goes."

"Frankly, I think there is more to the excellence of black kids today than just having this new generation of black kids exposed to knowledge through the Internet instead in knowledge-limited schoolbooks like they were in my Mother's generation. Sad to say, in the twentieth century there was some major survival of the fittest going on among black people. That was true in the United States and other western countries. It was even more tragically true in Africa.

"Now we have pretty well solved the things that held back—and killed, like my father—the blacks in the twentieth century. Twenty-first century black kids

149

are the children of survivors, and I think we have some echoes of survivor skills working for us too.

INTERVIEWER: "Thank you Mr. Eastliman, your story will be a terrific addition to what I am writing. I won't take any more of your time.

Euclid: "Not so fast! You are a black guy, and you must be about my age. How did you learn what you know? Do you have a few minutes to reciprocate with your story?

INTERVIEWER: "Absolutely. In fact, by the way, we are the same age. I was born January 9, 2000. You are only nine days older than I am. And I was not born in a hospital, I was born in a hut. My father died of AIDS when I was three, and I was one of the first kids to be cured by the new drugs. Mother was treated too, and she is still okay—but I know what you want to hear about is my education.

"I was neither schooled nor officially unschooled. When I got to be old enough for kindergarten the government and a lot of agencies had been trying to get a school going in our village for years. I have researched this across Africa and the truth is that there were huge efforts for decades to get schools going that followed the old model of the way the countries that colonized us did schooling. That seems backward to me, but old ideas die hard, as you know.

"By the time I was eight the only thing I had learned was a little bit of reading, writing and arithmetic that Mother showed me. The doctor who visited our village with the AIDS treatments also showed me some things about letters and numbers—she loved kids and enjoyed teaching us things. I think she was instrumental in getting the mobile project into our village.

"The mobile project was part of the beginning of the great African Renewal, as you may know. In our case, the project gave each person in the village a mobile that was a phone and had a small screen on which we could browse the Internet.

"Then the trend that really changed things for learning started, and I was exactly the right age to benefit from it the most. Funds that had been poured into planning and building the old kind of schools were diverted—a little at first and then a lot when the outcome was so effective—to giving stipends to teachers who would develop student groups for their subjects. Most of the teachers would make rounds to the neighborhoods and villages where there students were, usually twice a year. The rest of the time our teachers worked with us remotely through our mobiles. I was eleven when I had my first Mobile Teacher, as the program calls them.

Euclid: "Yes, of course. All over the world the project has been copied. My kids have mobile teachers for several subjects. But please, go on . . .

INTERVIEWER: "As a little kid with what was then a very simple mobile, I did do some fumbling around early on. When my first teacher visited our village, she had to spend most of her time showing the youngest of us how to find things to learn in the mobile. But we caught on quickly.

"Mr. Eastliman, I'll tell you what made the biggest difference. My own kids too have several Mobile Teachers and they learn most of their knowledge through their mobile devices. Their teachers are guides, individuals with whom they can discuss what they are learning and be challenged to learn more.

"The first Mobile Teachers were pioneers of this guidance and discoursing kind of teaching, using the open content knowledge as the source for the subject matter itself. But doing that was a lot harder when you and I were kids.

Euclid: "Please call me Euclid, and I think I can guess what you are going to say, but go ahead . . .

INTERVIEWER: "The big problem was nobody thought kids could dig into real knowledge.

Euclid: "That's right, of course!

INTERVIEWER: "The old colonial way was to expect the children only to learn the simple, limited ideas that the education experts thought appropriate.

Euclid: "Here in the USA, what the education experts did too. They set standards for subjects and expected us to march through them year-by-year, with everyone learning the same minimum stuff. There was a lot of celebration when black kids learned the minimum, and not much expectation that we would learn any more than that.

INTERVIEWER: "When our Mobile Teachers started showing us the content of scientific websites, historical research, language resources, arts and culture materials—well, it really created some outcry for a while. For me, though, it

151

worked just fine. My teachers worked with me individually, showing me around the Internet. When I got lost they would help me.

Euclid: "At the LUP, the same thing happened for us. We were lucky to be born when we were.

INTERVIEWER: Very lucky indeed.

Schooling Tomorrow

As the generation who are now children move—very quickly we can be sure—into their mobile tomorrow, it is increasingly silly to force them to submit to the kind of schooling created for their agrarian and industrial ancestors whose lives were locked down to land, neighborhood, industry, culture and country. Nonetheless, change is not expected by everybody. At the conclusion of his blog post about the presentation in which Todd Richmond predicts a perfect storm will drag the education sector into the future, Howard Rheingold reports this question that was discussed by those who attended the seminar where Richmond spoke:

> Will the non-educational reasons for schooling -- a place to park the kids while parents work and boot camp behavioral training for industrial-era employees and consumers -- prove to be the immovable object that stops the irresistible forces Richmond foresees?[28]

My own answer to that question is I do not know, but I am optimistic. With the hope that the object can be moved, I suggest these two steps:

The first step is to quit kidding ourselves about what schooling is in our times. Let us face up to the fact that, for other people's children and a least in part for our own, school is: *a place to park the kids while parents work and boot camp behavioral training for industrial-era employees and consumers.* When we have faced up to that actuality, we can work on figuring out whether parking them that way is a good or bad thing. We can quit pretending they are parked there to be scholars.

The second step is to move their scholarship into the cloud where the content of what is known by humankind networks as a commons to which each person in coming generations can connect in the mobile tomorrow. The

---

28   DIY Media Weblog, October 25, 2006. http://weblogs.annenberg.edu/diy/2006/10/ todd_richmond_on_open_educatio.html

knowledge is already online in that cloud; students need to be connected to be scholars. The mobile phone that browses the Internet will be the best connection for the new generation to that knowledge; that will be true no later than the end of the present decade.

Throughout this book, I have suggested in the future stories some ways that learning can improve in the mobile tomorrow. What will we do if the old way blows away? That may even be happening right now? What will the blueprint be if we can start over to build a system of learning in the digital age? Is there some reason we cannot demand a vision from our educators and our policy makers?

Or perhaps we should ignore stewards of the old ways and build learning from the bottom up, anew within the cloud—openly, interactively, using mobiles. We would let each learner exercise his or her role as the center of patterns within the networks of knowledge. Social networking among the ospheres of subjects would engage kids with the people and resources that cause the cloud to be smart.

What learning will be for the new generation is up to us. We can watch what happens or make something happen.

Gorillas Again

As she saw the library door begin to open, Alice pushed her mobile's mute button for the uniscreen to silence her Auntie Blanche. Then she punched the numbers to return the uniscreen to her teaching frequency.

Four women who appeared to be in their sixties came through the door. They walked over to Alice as she stood up and introduced themselves as the judges for the bioconservation competition. Alice explained that the students and parents would be arriving soon and showed the judges where the kids would make their presentations and where the judges should sit. The four older women were taking their positions behind the judges' table as once again the door opened.

A crowd of kids and adults started coming in. Alice ushered parents and student observers toward the audience area and asked the student competitors to gather around her so she could review the rules and logistics. There were two teams who would make presentations. All of the members of the teams were bioconservation students she had been teaching for the past four months. They ranged in age from eleven to sixteen-years-old, with younger and older students on each team. Alice did not discriminate on age in accepting students into her teaching programs. She judged applicants on what they knew and their enthusiasm for the subject.

The presentation by the first team of five students was on the topic of "Prairie Rodent Preservation." They first filled the uniscreen with compelling images of cute little rodents nibbling grass as two of the students alternated describing the individual rodents depicted. Next they opened a frequency to Mongolia where three children from a nomad herding family showed the gerbils they were raising. One of Alice's students then talked in some detail about the preservation of gerbils as pets.

The second presentation team, also with five members, next prepared to present on their topic of "Communicating with Gorillas" They began by setting up a very large cage that they had made out of the cardboard from some packing boxes. One of the younger team members—he is eleven-years-old—then discussed the Aframomum spice that keeps the heart of a gorilla healthy. After that, a girl who is fourteen narrated images displayed on the uniscreens of the team's recent trip to the Bronx Zoo Congo Gorilla Forest.

The student team leader, a thirteen-year-old girl, then explained the multi-gorilla-game they had helped the Bronx staff devise in which gorillas could use simple mobiles to play a banana-counting game on screens in their habitats. "We are going to try to make that happen live," she said proudly.

Before long, the uniscreen was divided into four sections and a gorilla could be seen in each. All of the gorillas were touching pictures of bananas on the screens of oversized mobile each had in his or her hand. The same image that was on their mobiles was projected on the wall of each gorilla habitat. Now and then a real banana would plop on to the trough in front of one of the projected screens. "The two at the top are in the Bronx," the leader explained. "The one in the bottom right is in a wildlife park in China and the one on the bottom left is a gorilla they call Bozo who lives in the Aframomum Hothouse in Rwanda. Bozo always wins."

The judges and the audience watched the game intently for a few minutes. As the leader had predicted, soon Bozo had nine bananas and none of the others had more than three.

The leader said brightly, "Would you like to meet Bozo up close?"

Before anyone had a chance to respond, Bozo appeared inside of the cardboard box. "He is only a hologram," the leader said, "but we thought he needed a cage so you would not be frightened. We are now ready to answer the judges questions," the girl concluded as her team lined up next to the cage and facing the judges' table.

Some time went by as the eight-hundred-pound gorilla inside the cardboard cage began eating his bananas one-by-one. Finally, one of the judges who was a veteran teacher spoke up and congratulated the team for its originality. She then asked the students what they felt was the most important factor in the ecoconservation of gorillas.

The team leader said, "The mobile in my hand."

The veteran teacher respond, "Why do you think that? How about the gorillas themselves, all the people and facilities at the gorillas projects in Rwanda and China and the Bronx, and your own teacher? That thing in your hand is just a few buttons and chips."

The team leader said with just an edge of sharpness in her voice, "The answer to what you say is very easy." She clicked a couple of times on her mobile and Bozo disappeared. "With this in my hand there is no eight hundred pound gorilla."

Alice thought to herself, "I've got to introduce that girl to Auntie Blanche."

Some Gorillas to Notice Now

In writing this book I have tried to make the dreary subject of education failure more lively to read by having some fun with the future, by mixing in some sparkle with the word intertwingle and by introducing the obviousness of the eight-hundred pound gorillas that are being ignored in education. For this concluding discussion of education's ten-year turning of its backside toward the digital dawn it is going to take a few more gorillas.

The eight-hundred pound gorilla in the room with education political planners, almost all school board meetings and fidgeting in the corner of the education industry's profit planners is the big ape who throws his banana peels at the education-as-always folks and roars: "Why would you humans wait another twenty years to let your kids do these digital things?"

We should all share that gorilla's frustration, and be doing something about it! Everything except the gorilla holograph in the story just told can be done as I write this book, and done much more effectively very soon with mobiles already coming down the pipe.

There are lots more big gorillas in the education forest. We will look in on five of them—all big guys who are obvious reminders of major badly overdue digital doings we should be demanding for educating the young generation and the kids after that.

Before we drop in on these concluding gorillas, it is good to be clear about why they have been so difficult to see, even though they have long since begun pacing in full view in the places where are kids are supposed to be getting educated. For one thing, all of us are somewhat overwhelmed by the thought of changing—or worse, abandoning—our schools. Whether we live in the most prosperous areas of the developed world, the promising environs of the developing world or the least prosperous or hopeful regions of our planet, we all have deep seated education traditions. Change is difficult; people want their kids to enjoy the parts of their growing years that they remember as happy and times of learning. Yet they need to keep in mind that their kids are headed into a new kind of world, and that to some extent they are already there as they use the Internet and their mobile phones. For their sake we must be willing to make changes.

We are also often given the impression from educators that they are doing what they can to use the Internet in learning. Although there are individual people and schools that reach somewhat into the cloud, in no real sense has education embraced the digital world, especially below the college level.

157

The following are five glaring omissions to fix—places to start now to open the way. There is more to do, as suggested throughout these pages, but these are five basic starting interactions with their future that every student should and could be exercising right now.

Open content

As a class of students sits with textbooks open all to the same page and discusses the main point in each of the four paragraphs on the page, an eight-hundred pound gorilla sits in their midst waving around his mobile phone. On the screen of his mobile its web browser has listed links to several online sources for information on the main point in first paragraph on the textbook page.

The gorilla is yelling: "Hey humans, click on these links and you will learn more. What you learn will be more up-to-date and will link out to interesting related stuff. You will understand the ideas better. You won't get bored."

The teacher does not hear. The kids pretend they do not have mobiles in their pockets. The preparation for a standard test continues. Everyone in the room knows that if the students learn the main point in each of the four paragraphs that they will score well on the next test and everyone will be happy: the teacher, the principle, the politicians, their parents and the kids themselves.

The gorilla is not happy. The huge primate jumps up and down, spinning in circles waving his mobile as its ringtone plays the old song *Yes We Have No Bananas* at full volume. No one notices.

Long ago a system was created to deliver knowledge to students in schools that were scattered far and wide by geography. The system assumed that when a student enrolled in a school that the student's sources of knowledge would be the teachers it has hired and the books it supplied. Today geographic separation has become irrelevant and that formula is badly out of date, yet the presumption and practice remain. The teachers and books located in any school today can provide only a small percentage of what is openly available online.

The content a student is instructed to study should be open. It should not be limited to a textbook interpretation and/or a teacher's version. The student should be able to interact with the online resources available for the subject.

In the same vein, educators, students, parents and policy makers should promote the opening online of university and other institutional knowledge resources for academic subjects. The trend toward opening learning resources has begun but needs to be completed. There is no longer a justification for ivy walls to enclose knowledge. Although the institutions walled by ivy may feel entitled

158

to be paid for their resources, that is unlikely to happen. Instead their walled off intellectual assets are far more likely to lose relevance by being disconnected from the online commons. Walled off knowledge cannot intertwingle with other knowledge, teachers or learners.

In any event, the opening of content from the student side will immediately enrich what they can learn. A little supplementary research for school assignments is not learning from open content—not intertwingling. To enable the new learning potential fo the 21st century, every student needs to have in his or her hand a mobile device that browses the Internet. That browsing must become central to school work for schools to remain relevant.

Long tail learning

Our next gorilla is a sporty fellow. He spends his time skateboarding down power law curves. The curves are perfect for his sport. They start extremely high, drop very steep and fast and after that they descend gently into the distance, some say forever.

Among the gorilla's favorite power law curves is the one made at Amazon.com by the books it has for sale on its website. The head is what the high part of the power law curve is called. For Amazon.com books the head is very high and the drop really sharp to the beginning of the long tail, which is what the gentle descent into the distance is called. For Amazon, the head is the most popular books—the best sellers and a few hundred others that sell very well. The long tail has many thousands of books, starting with books that sell some copies and descending through many, many books that sell a fewer and fewer copies, then a handful, then just two or one.

This gorilla refuses to skateboard on school knowledge curves because he will tell you, "Education learning chops off the long tail. Learning comes to a halt looking over that cliff, and I am not about to skateboard off the edge into that oblivion of no ideas!" The gorilla will explain that what children are expected to learn in most schools is nothing more than the head of the power curve of knowledge. The long tail of all the subjects are chopped off.

When any subject—say for example mammal biology—is put into the Internet it forms what Dr. OO calls an osphere. That would be an osphere of mammal biology all interconnected like the blogosphere. Because it is in a network the knowledge about mammal biology would form a power law curve, acting just the way the books do in Amazon.com. There would be a few big things about mammal biology that would form the head of the curve and then

159

the rest of the knowledge about smaller and more detailed things would go off on a gentle curve that forms a very long tail. As the skateboard gorilla will tell you, in schools that curve will get chopped of at the head and the long tail will be lost. The students get high scores on tests when they only learn a few things. If they could study on the open Internet they could start with the important stuff in the head, and if they had the time and curiosity they could go out into the long tail and learn more connected ideas.

Something important that has been learned in recent years from network theory is that small-world networks contents follow the power law. The brick and mortar world often does not follow that curve. A bookstore has a limit to its shelf space, so typically it only stocks the head of the curve: best sellers and other books that sell very well. You are not going to find books on specialized and detailed topics in the bookstore in your mall. Since Amazon does not have a shelf space limit it can offer the full range of books—it can and does include the long tail.

Education publications such as printed textbooks cannot physically offer the long tail of ideas that our information rich times offer to and demand of our young people. Part of the reason the publishers are straining our children's lumbar regions by imposing heavier and heavier textbooks is to try to overcome that failure.

"Why," grumbles the skateboard gorilla, "don't they save the children's backs and let them use the long tail device in their pockets? I'd love to put a banana peel in the tracks of those school textbook committees—slide them kicking and screaming into the digital future!"

DIY: Do It Yourself

A classroom of twenty eleventh grade students in a suburban school in the Midwestern United States is given this assignment from the state social studies standards of what students are supposed to learn:

> Describe how the perspectives of cultural groups helped to cre-
> ate political action groups such as: a. The National Association for the
> Advancement of Colored People (NAACP).

The teacher gives the students a list of materials, including some book excerpts on the school system website, that they are assigned to read to prepare for the essay they must write. They will be graded on how well they understand the materials they are assigned to read.

The eight-hundred pound gorilla who is leaning in the corner next to the teacher begins beating his chest with his fists. "Rotten bananas," he screams, "let the kids do it themselves! They are already making culture online every day. This assignment is a century out of date! Rotten, rotten bananas." He slumps into the corner and dusts some chalk dust off of his elbow as he mutters, "Good grief and leaping slugs—chalk! These kids should be communicating in pixels!! I don't see how they put up with this stuff."

Howard Rheingold described the kids the gorilla was sympathizing with in the answer wrote in January 2007 to John Brockman's annual question put to a widespread community of thinkers and published on Edge.org. Brockman's 2007 question was "What are you optimistic about?" Rheingold's answer was: "The tools for cultural production and distribution are in the pockets of 14 year olds." Rheingold continued:

> The eager adoption of web publishing, digital video production and online video distribution, social networking services, instant messaging, multiplayer role-playing games, online communities, virtual worlds, and other Internet-based media by millions of young people around the world demonstrates the strength of their desire — unprompted by adults — to learn digital production and communication skills. Whatever else might be said of teenage bloggers, dorm-room video producers, or the millions who maintain pages on social network services like MySpace and Facebook, it cannot be said that they are passive media consumers.[29]

The passive learning that lingers in classrooms is increasingly unendurable for the new generation. As they walk out of their school doors they pull the mobile tomorrow out of their pockets and switch to the DIY virtual world.

Money, work and enthusiasm from the education sector should be poured into do it yourself learning venues for the new generation. Any student with a mobile phone, for example, should be able to practice mathematics with the device—there is no excuse for that not happening unless, as some grumpy gorilla might say, because then what would happen to the money and people now thrown at the old print and drill sorts of math education?

If the new generation is doing everything else online—and increasingly

---

29 Howard Rheingold. Quoted from his comment Edge.org, http://www.smartmobs.com/archive/2007/01/01/the_tools_of_cu....html

with their mobile devices—they should be allowed to learn that way too.

Games

The first generation of video and then digital game players are in their thirties in the early 21st century. It is their children who are now moving up through the school grades. We are now two generations into the game phenomenon and a very old eight-hundred pound gorilla wearing a tie with the initials DK is wailing outside the school door: "Why haven't they let the games in?"

Donkey Kong is asking a question that has recently been getting a lot of high-powered attention. Here, for example, is part of the introduction to a 2006 article titled The Play of Imagination: *Beyond the Literary Mind* written by Douglas Thomas and John Seely Brown:

> These games combine the power of traditional forms of roleplaying games with a rich, textured graphical framework. The result has been the emergence of game spaces which provide players with new and unusual opportunities for learning. As these games become increasingly popular and as they begin to approximate large scale social systems in size and nature, they have also become spaces where play and learning have merged in fundamental ways, where players have become deeply enmeshed in the practices and cultures of interactive play, collaboration, and learning. More important is the idea that the kind of learning that happens in these spaces is fundamentally different from the learning experiences associated with standard pedagogical practice.[30]

Appreciation of gaming as learning is not only cutting edge. It is a well established learning method outside of schools. Games are doing significant teaching and training in the corporate sector and the military. A Business Week article in March 2006 described a Cold Stone Creamery game that trained staff to serve ice cream, video games used by the military for training, a drag and drop training game for Canon repairmen that teaches them where to put replacement parts, and this report on Cisco game training:

> Cisco rolled out six new training games -- some of them designed to teach technicians how to build a computer network. It's hard to

---

30 Douglas Thomas and John Seely Brown. The Play of Imagination: Beyond the Literary Mind (PDF), September 16, 2006. http://www.johnseelybrown.com/

imagine a drier subject. Not so in the virtual world. In one Cisco game, players must put the network together on Mars. In a sandstorm. "Our employees learn without realizing they are learning," says Field. Sounds suspiciously like fun.

Massively multiplayer games, the enormous virtual world called Second Life and other virtual participatory venues are a large, arriving area of great importance. Educators and all of us who wish to help the new generation into the future should become informed and active in the field.

For starters, big old Donkey Kong has a demand we all should join: "Let's get games on to student mobile phones so they can learn from them in class, on the bus and/or at home?" If DK has the vision to understand the gift of mobile game learning, we humans can surely see it too.

Mobile

The bell has rung to change periods and students are beginning to file into school Computer Lab 4. The school is proud to have a four rooms dedicated to computers. Called labs, the rooms are set up with rows of tables five across and five deep for a total of twenty-five computers. Because classes are usually at least thirty students, some of the computers are shared. Each table has a chair behind it and there are ten extra chairs in the room to use for sharing.

There is an eight-hundred pound gorilla sitting on (squashing, actually) some packing boxes at the back of the room. He signals one of the boys who is coming into the room to come over.

The boy looks around nervously then walks over to stand in front of the gorilla. "What do you want?" he whispers. "I don't want to get in trouble."

"Don't worry about that," the gorilla laughs, "nobody ever notices me."

"Guess not," the boy replies.

"Listen, kid," the gorilla says quietly, "how much computer time do you get at school every day? I'm just curious."

"Two hours," was his answer, "one during this period and another starts at 2:13 this afternoon."

"Do you use the same computer both times?" the gorilla asked.

"Of course not, the computers are in different rooms. But I have my own file that I keep on a server in the school center.

The gorilla then asked, "Do you have a computer at home?"

"Sure, I've got a laptop. It's wireless and I take it with me a lot of places.

But they don't like it when I bring it here. I can't use it in class. I am supposed to use my lab time for work on one of these computers."

The gorilla then persisted in his questions until he learned that the boy's files on the school server were protected by a firewall so the boy could not access them outside the school and work with them from home. The boy further explained that research on the Internet at school did not work very well because a lot of the Internet was blocked.

The gorilla finally said, "I have one other question: do you have a mobile phone."

The boy say very quietly, "Are you trying to get me in trouble?"

"No," the big ape said with a very large grin, "remember they ignore me, and when I am talking to you they ignore you too. They don't even see you."

"Well then," the boy said, "take a look at this." He pulled a high end smart phone out of his pants pocket and handed it to the gorilla.

The gorilla took the phone and pushed quite a few buttons. Then he started laughing. "I see you play Donkey Kong. I am actually quite good at it. I can even beat Kong himself. We have a massively multiplayer eight-hundred pound gorilla game, you know. Sitting in rooms not being noticed gets awfully boring. We use our mobiles to play, and Donkey Kong is at the twenty-third level. I am fifteen up from that. Kid, would you like to sit in on one of our games?"

"Sure," the boy said. He watched the gorilla program something into his phone. Then he handed it back to the boy.

"Click in at 4:30 this afternoon," the gorilla said.

"Way, way cool," the boy whispered. "Thank you!"

As the boy started to turn away he heard a woman's voice from directly behind him. The voice said, "Please introduce me to your gorilla."

Spinning about the boy saw the school principal and a woman he had never seen before. The boy blurted out, "I thought you couldn't see him, or me either."

The woman spoke up. "I am the president of the board of education. We have been hearing rumors of gorillas being seen in many of our schools. Something happened today that we don't understand, but suddenly they have become visible. I rushed over here to see this one when your principal here called to say you were talking with him. Is he dangerous?"

"I don't think so," the boy said.

"Do you know his name?" she asked.

"Bozo," the gorilla replied.

"Well, Bozo," do you realize you are squashing a pile of our new desktop computers?" the president of the board of education said.

"I know madam," Bozo answered politely, "but they are obsolete. Not very comfortable either. But would you like to sit on a couple?" Bozo slid two side-by-side boxes over near the president of the board of education, and she sat down.

As the boy and the principal—and then many other students and faculty from the school— gathered around, watching and listening, Bozo and the president of the board of education discussed the use of mobile devices for learning. On that day, which was to become known as international *Gorillas Are Good Day*, across the world the eight-hundred pound gorillas who had been sitting in schoolrooms for years were suddenly noticed.

Because of what was learned from the gorillas, education was not dragged kicking and screaming into the digital future. Instead everyone worked together to make certain every young person had a mobile that interacted with the cloud for learning. Soon the gorillas spent most of their time playing massively multiape games, and sometimes they let kids play too.

And everyone lived happily ever after in the intertwingled mobile tomorrow.

ABOUT THE AUTHOR

Judy Breck is a blogger who lives in New York City. Her home node online is GoldenSwamp.com.

www.ingramcontent.com/pod-product-compliance
Lightning Source LLC
Chambersburg PA
CBHW031935190326
41519CB00007B/547